The H.A.R.V.A.R.D. EFFECT

Communicate to Elevate

T.D. Jakes once said, "Don't let my talent take me where my character can't keep me." I want to acknowledge my mother, Lajaune Bryant, and my father, Les Brown, for supporting me through all the character-building experiences that I have encountered in life.

This book is dedicated to my son, Honor Phoenix Brown. If I can be as great of a parent as the parents I have been blessed with, it would be a joy of unspeakable value.

This book is also dedicated to the students of life who never graduate from a prestigious university. May this curriculum help you graduate to unimaginable heights.

-John-Leslie Brown

Copyright © 2016 by John Leslie Brown

The H.A.R.V.A.R.D EFFECT
www.HarvardEffect.com

All rights reserved. No part of this publication may be reproduced, distributed, or transmitted in any form or by any means, including photocopying, recording, or other electronic or mechanical methods, without the prior written permission of the publisher, except in the case of brief quotations embodied in critical reviews and certain other noncommercial uses permitted by copyright law. For permission requests, write to the publisher, addressed "Attention: Permissions Coordinator," at info@beyondpublishing.net

Quantity sales special discounts are available on quantity purchases by corporations, associations, and others. For details, contact the publisher at the address above.

Orders by U.S. trade bookstores and wholesalers.

Email info@BeyondPublishing.net

First Beyond Publishing soft cover edition December 2016

The Beyond Publishing Speakers Bureau can bring authors to your live event. For more information or to book an event, contact the Beyond Publishing Speakers Bureau speak@BeyondPublishing.net

The Author can be reached directly at HarvardEffect.com

Manufactured and printed in the United States of America distributed globally by BeyondPublishing.net

New York | Los Angeles | London | Sydney

10 9 8 7 6 5 4 3 2 1   ISBN 978-0-9987292-7-5

ACKNOWLEDGEMENTS

To my publishing advisor, Michael Butler. Thank you for all your guidance through this enormous task. Renée Daniel, thank you for your hard work to make this project the best it can be. Timothy Thomas, your video inspired me not to hold back.

To everyone who pre-ordered this book. Jessica Noe, you are a fire-starter. Keep being a shining example. As I grow, we grow together. Thank you for sharing your dynasty with me.

I would also like to acknowledge:

    Dwight Pledger
    Evelyn Polk
    Artisse Sanders
    Timothy Thomas
    Beth Brown
    Patrick Artis
    Pamela Etzwiler
    Patricia Alberino
    Charity Brown
    Billie Back
    Jennifer Moore
    LeeAnn Brown
    Michael Brown
    Michael Brown
    Kathleen Tisher
    BreaCole Streng
    Lawrence Clark
    Lorraine Szydlowski
    Kayla Farrell cyedmonta
    Wilson Charlene Lewis
    Cheryl Hamilton
    ARASH GHIASI
    Lynn Arnett

I would like to thank my grandmother, Mamie Brown, and my grandfather, John Greene. This generation is reaping the benefits of your courage. Mamie Brown, my grandma, taught my dad, Les Brown, what the true meaning of compassion is. My maternal grandfather taught my mother, Lajaune Bryant, what the essence of successful entrepreneurship is all about. Two of the most influential people in my life are my grandfather and my grandmother, whom I have never met.

My parents were never married, and their parents never crossed paths, but these unknown motivators to the world helped keep me motivated daily, because of the values they instilled in me. I hope this body of work will make them proud, and that I live out the legacy by honoring their names and values, and that they enjoy the feeling of pride from beyond this realm.

One of the world's best educators in my book is Marva N. Collins. She mentored me, and I will never forget it. I can still taste her banana pancakes when I think of them and would have loved to have said goodbye at her funeral service, but her legacy with me will never die.

To my brothers and sisters who have helped me grow from boy to man to father. Thank you, Karissa Campbell, for being there and driving to Boston on your birthday for this historic occasion. I thank you, Patrick, Tia, Ona, Serena, Calvin, Sumaya. Each of you have been more than a sibling. You are my role models. Thank you to my Aunt Margaret and Uncle Alex for helping groom me as a young man.

Thank you, Myles Munroe, Bishop T.D. Jakes, Jim Rohn, Denzel Washington, Brian Tracy, Greg Reid, Gail Kingsbury, Luther Vandross, Suzanne De Passe, Diana Ross, Tracee Ellis Ross, Della Reese, Omarion, Kam Talbert, Joseph Gordon-Levitt, Dr. Johnny Coleman, Levon Davis, Gladys Knight, Ice Cube, and Krs One for not allowing your celebrity to get in the way of mentoring the next generation. There is not a day that goes by that I don't reflect on the positive seeds that planted in my heart at an early age as they continue to sprout new growth.

I also want to dedicate this book to a group of people who have a powerful bond with my spirit thatcan't be expressed in words. Patricia Henley (Aunty Patty), Kam Talbert, Duriel Porter, and Curtis Burton.

Akia Taylor, you are the best coach ever. Furthermore, Dolly Amaya, Dean Lambert, and the Harvard University Leadership students who I am proud to now call friends.

My extended thanks goes to my foundational influences: Sami Douglas, Donald Wilson Bush, and Azua. Furthermore, my awesome mother, Solshock, and, my hero; my dad, Les Brown. You both taught me the proper way to fly. I am your student. I apologize for the many times I have let you down, but thank you for always caring enough to help me lift myself up from mediocrity. I am your student.

This book is part of my assignment that you gave me as a child. Thank you for giving me a Harvard-quality education in success and entrepreneurship.

Thank you, La Jaune Bryant, the world's most resourceful mother, for all your patience. To Berny Dhorman and September, it's our time! Mr. Robert Simpson, thank you for trusting me with the world's most beautiful director to one day call my wife. Mrs. Lena Simpson, your chant inspired me more than you can imagine. Thank you to my beautiful fiancée, for saying yes, and for being so understanding and inspirational.

Last but now least, I want to thank those of you in advance preordering, participating, and contributing to the process of this book.

If you have any, ideas, notes, pictures, videos, or exercises that can help elevate the strategies in this book, please email me at johnlesliebrown@ harvardeffect.com. This sneak peek is a work in progress. Immediately before reading this book, please join our Harvard Effect private Facebook group, and upload all assignments to the group as you complete them.

The action steps in the book must be completed in the sequence provided, in order to have massive effect. All edits and video blog submissions must be completed before February 1, 2017.

The old keys to success no longer open the new locks on the doors of opportunity that many high achievers must walk through daily. A key has no expiration date, and it can never get old. However, once an old door has a new lock, the keys that once worked become ineffective.

Some of us get upset with the door, instead of assigning blame to the keys. The

H.A.R.V.A.R.D. Effect gives you a new set of keys; one that can open the doors that you thought were impossible to enter.

Go to www.HarvardEffect.com to find bonus video and audio material that is not in the book. This will help all types of learners fully take advantage of these keys. Each chapter and assignment will be listed in the online course at www.harvardeffect.com. Join our private community and share your achievements with us.

CONTENTS

AUTHORS FORWARD: The Dynasty Leap 9
Early Admissions- Growing Up In Greatness 12

1. Orientation Chapter
   Hundred Year Plan 35
   Unlock The Gates of Capacity 39
   Travelator Pitch 44
   Boost Your Mental Software 52
   Reverse Accountability 59

2. Freshman Chapter
   Allow Yourself to Fall 66
   Courage is an Ancient Currency 79
   Mastery Loves Company 87

3. Sophomore Chapter
   Resource Management 92
   Own Your Mental Equity 94
   Maximize Your Down Time 104
   Raise Your Relationship Capital 111

4. Junior Chapter
   Virtualize Yourself 126
   World-wide Learning Curve 127
   Borderless Wikinomics 134
   The Social Credibility Movement 137

5. Senior Chapter
   Acknowledge Your Journey 143
   Ribbon Recognition 143
   The Talk of Touch 149
   Sounds of Success 153

6. Master's Chapter
   Rise to the Occasion 161
   Up on Bended Knee 163
   Above The Wave..169

	Call to Elevation 172
7.	Doctor's Chapter
	Dwell in gratitude 173
	The Gold In Rush 175
	File of Thankruptcy 176

The H.A.R.V.A.R.D. EFFECT

Communicate to Elevate

THE DYNASTY LEAP

Success is the only choice. The sentence jumped out at me from my Facebook messages. This message contained one of the most phenomenal opportunities of my life. "I am contacting you on behalf of Harvard University. We are interested in having you speak at one of our events. Please get back to me as soon as possible." Instantly, I felt a deep anchor of honor.

Part of me wanted to doubt its credibility. Write it off as a prank. A spam email, perhaps. However, a much larger part of me knew that I had earned that right. Have you ever had an opportunity that made all the struggles you've endured seem as though it had all been worth it? Well, that is exactly how I felt at the moment I learned that I would speak at one of the most influential universities on the planet.

Each year, over 30,000 students apply for a place at Harvard, but, sadly, fewer than six percent of those applicants earn their rite of passage. Those who do, however, are set for a life of prosperity. 98 percent of Harvard students graduate and go on to achieve something special.

Since I had never even finished community college, I began to imagine what my life would look like if I had a Harvard education. How would that have affected my career prospects and lifestyle goals? What about the lives of my loved ones? How would their lives be different if they had such a prestigious start in life?

Harvard breeds leadership, and the dynasty is timeless. Presidents, Nobel Prize winners, and Nobel Laureates have walked through its corridors and been molded by its prestige. Joining this community of high-achievers means you'll study beside a select group of young men and women, many of whom are set up for greatness from birth and go on to shape the world. Even Harvard's dropouts go on to become billionaires; Bill Gates and Mark Zuckerberg—the founders of Microsoft and Facebook, respectively—are two particularly prominent examples.

Now, it was finally my chance to impact the next generation of high-achievers.

Imagine you could speak to the next leaders of our time. What advice would you give them? What stories would you share that could shape the minds of our next heads of state? How would you inspire our leaders of the future?

///

My grandfather, John Greene, knew all about the H.A.R.V.A.R.D. Effect. Growing up in the Mississippi, there was poverty and abuse in his household that he rarely spoke of. He saved every penny he could earn, packed up all his belongings, and, at the early age of 13, moved, alone, to Detroit. He would never see his family again.

When I think about what my grandfather must have felt in his heart as he boarded that train, heading towards an unfamiliar place with limited resources, I can sum it up in seven words: there's got to be a better way.

He found that better way when he opened one of the first minority-owned businesses in that area, a soul food restaurant, named Greens BBQ. I can still remember my childhood days in the homely eatery. It may not have looked like much from the outside, but, inside, the type of food served couldn't be replicated in fast food joints. This food, my grandfather's food, was prepared with a very important ingredient: love. Ribs, greens, ox tails, you name it, every last drop of my grandfather's love was poured into it.

My mother grew up in that restaurant and, later, helped to cook and take orders. Working in the family business taught her the fundamental lessons of life. She didn't have it easy, you see. At just 17 years old, she gave birth to my sister, Tia. Despite this initial struggle, as well as struggling with the loss of her mother just a few years after my sister was born, ten years later, she was making a decent living.

Still, my mother carved her way through life with all the determination and drive that she was bound to inherit. She was, after all, John Bryant's daughter. She made it through life alone until, one day, she attended a church service where there was a guest speaker. As my mom had entered a little late, she did not catch the speaker's name as he was introduced. Something about the mysterious man's voice stirred up something deep within her. Since the room was packed, she couldn't really see him, so she decided to stand up on a chair.

Over the heads of the gathered crowds, this strong, tenacious woman caught her first glimpse of the man who would become a dynamic inspiration to her. His name was Les Brown. Very few people knew his name then, but, when they met, she knew that his voice could make a difference.

Over time, they began dating, and my mother was one of the first people fighting to get his message out there. One day, feeling despondent, he talked to my mom about moving into a different industry, maybe giving up as a public speaker and going into sales.

My mom looked at him with absolute certainty and firmly stated, "Les, you can't do that."

"Why not?" He asked.

The simple answer cemented his path in life. "Because your mouth has gold in it. You have to use your voice. You have to share your stories with the world."

As usual, my mother was right. Les Brown, my father, went on to become one of the top five speakers on the planet. His voice has made an impact on a countless number of lives. While my mom was pregnant with me, she would put my dad's motivational tapes in her Walkman. Determined that I would be programmed for greatness even while in the womb, she would take the headphones and put them over her stomach, hoping that my newly formed ears would make sense of his words. I like to think it worked.

Thanks to my grandfather's successful path in Detroit, that was the city in which I was born in 1984. My mom hyphenated my name, John-Leslie, because she wanted me to be named after both paternal influences: my father and my grandfather. Many years have passed since I visited Greens BBQ for the first time, but I still remember clambering up the stairs to discover the shining dance floor and magnificent pool table. It was beautiful to me.

At the time, I didn't know my grandfather's story; I didn't know that the restaurant was a vehicle for him to start a new family, a place where everyone would eventually work at as they came of age. I had no clue how difficult it is to be an entrepreneur. As I reflect on my childhood and remember my amazement at our family business, I realize that my grandfather, who never got any awards in academia, was the first person to teach me about the H.A.R.V.A.R.D. Effect .

///

To make it to the big stage, you must start with something small. That small restaurant provided for my mom and her siblings, and, even after my grandfather had passed away, our family was still living on his legacy.

It's amazing to think back on just how much he achieved; just a Mississippi boy with no experience or qualification in business. He didn't need experience. He didn't need qualifications. John Bryant knew his community. Loved it, in fact. Part of his proceeds funded the local baseball teams. My grandfather may not have been famous, and he may not have been a millionaire, but he still found a way to give back.

The main force behind the H.A.R.V.A.R.D. Effect is one of philanthropy. It is about executing the necessary strategies that will put you in a position to empower others. Sure, there are a lot of books that can teach you how to gain your own success but the book you hold in your hands now is designed to inspire you to move past your own achievements. With this book, you can be an influence to generations, leaving a legacy that will empower others long after you depart from this world. That is what living is all about.

Growing Up in Greatness

You could say that greatness has been programmed into me from birth.

Since my grandfather, father, and mother were such strong, trailblazing individuals, it was obvious that I would achieve something spectacular in life. Only, there is a fourth person to add to the equation: My grandmother.

By the time I was nine months old, my mother and I had moved to Miami, Florida, to live with my dad's adoptive mother, Ms. Mamie Brown. My grandmother never went beyond a third-grade education. She never started her own business, nor did she travel much. Her life was simple; however, she, too, was a master at the H.A.R.V.A.R.D. Effect and was, perhaps, my most influential professor.

Ms. Mamie Brown had one dream. She never married and lived her life alone, but that didn't bother her. Her dream was to become a mother. Throughout her life, she adopted seven children, even though she had no partner to help her. She loved every single one with all she had. To this day, I am astonished by the mindset my grandmother must have had to take care of seven babies who had no one else to count on for love.

My dad, Leslie, and his twin brother, Weslie, were among the first babies she adopted. They resided in a part of Miami known as Liberty City. Ironically, liberty was hard to find in Liberty City. If you wanted liberty, you needed to catch a jitney or bus to Miami Beach.

At least, that is what Ms. Mamie Brown had to do to take care of all her adopted children. This was the 1950s, and the only decent work Ms. Mamie Brown could find was either as a cafeteria worker or as a maid and cook for the wealthy people who lived on Miami Beach. My grandmother never let that hold her back, and, true to form, she stepped up to her role and did whatever it took to provide for her family.

Even though Ms. Mamie Brown never made a lot of money, her mindset and skillset made it possible for a new dynasty to emerge. Her whatever-it-takes attitude towards life and fulfilling her dream as a mother is what eventually gave me the opportunity to write this book. John Bryant and Mamie Brown are, essentially, co-authors in the

H.A.R.V.A.R.D. Effect curriculum. Without their sacrifices in Florida and Michigan, I would never have had the opportunity to set the microphone on fire in my own life.

Growing up, my dad was the toughest kid in the house, but that didn't stop him being vulnerable at times. He didn't know that he was adopted until one day, when he was playing football with some kids outside. While my dad was boasting about a touchdown he had made, one of the kids shouted, "Shut up, fool! That's why you're adopted." At first, my dad didn't believe it, but, when he went into the house and asked my grandma if it was true, there was no point in a denial.

Contrary to what you would expect, this experience only made his heart open more. He saw how hard his mother was working to provide for them and that made him truly appreciate the chance he'd been given in life.

Not long thereafter, my father went with my grandmother to help clean the home of a local family. My dad enjoyed it, because the Suderski family had a son the same age, David. As fate would have it, this particular day happened to be David's sixteenth birthday. While my dad and David were talking in the office, Mr. Suderski came in to give his son two presents, and, as he did so, said, "One present is much more valuable than the other."

As David unwrapped the first gift, he discovered that it contained a key.

"This is yours, Son. I hope you enjoy it," smiled Mr. Suderski, explaining that it was the key to his David's very own boat. Think about how little Leslie must have felt. He had never seen his father. Never hugged him. Never even knew him. But, now, he was witnessing David Suderski's father give him a boat for his birthday.

That is the type of liberty that just did not exist in Liberty City. My father was learning firsthand what it means to grow up in the gutter, and what it means to grow up in greatness.

As you would imagine, David was truly excited about the boat, but

Mr. Suderski still had another gift lying in wait. One that he claimed was even more valuable. "Son, this gift that I share with you now is precious. It has helped me to build my fortune, and, if you can study and master this, you'll be set for life." Hidden behind his back, he slowly revealed a record. It was one of the first motivational albums ever produced and mass-marketed: *The Strangest Secret In*

The World, by Earl Nightingale.

David pretended to be excited about the record, but, when his father left the room, he tossed it in the trashcan. My dad saw this and, bewildered, asked, "Why would you do that? Your dad said that was worth more than the boat."

"It doesn't matter. After he dies, I inherit everything anyway," replied David.

Young Leslie was intrigued by the record. He wanted to find out about the strangest secret in the world that helped the Suderski family build their dynasty. He asked David if it was okay to take it out of the trash and if, when he came over, he could listen to it on his record player. David agreed. And the Brown Dynasty was born.

The First Family of Motivation

Earl Nightingale — the Dean of Personal Development, as he was known — became the

H.A.R.V.A.R.D. Effect professor for my dad during the 1950s. When he was listening to *The Strangest Secret in the World*, he had no idea that this one recording would change the course of his future.

Earl Nightingale was a radio host who went on to receive the Golden Gavel award from Toastmasters International. After reading a book called *Think and Grow Rich* by Napoleon Hill at the age of 29, young Nightingale figured out an answer for the deep curiosity he had about life. He wondered about the true meaning. Even in his twenties, he was exploring his self-worth and doing his best to figure out his purpose.

"Success," stated Earl Nightingale, "is the progressive realization of a worthy ideal." My dad would hear these words as he watched his adoptive mother clean the Suderski estate floors and reflect on his own worthy ideal.

"Throughout all history, the great wise men, teachers, philosophers, and prophets have disagreed with one another on many different things. It's only on this one point that they are in complete and unanimous agreement."

Young Leslie listened in amazement as the Dean of Personal Development whispered the strangest secret in the world. That secret, said Earl Nightingale, is this: we become what we think about.

Leslie was captivated by Nightingale, perhaps because of my father's reputation of being stupid. He was held back in school twice and labeled "educable mentally retarded," — having a below-average mental function. His friends used to call him D.T., short for a dumb twin. As he listened in awe to the timeless wisdom of Earl Nightingale, this young boy had no idea that as a man, he would join Earl Nightingale in the Speaker's Hall of Fame and would, himself, go on to receive the Golden Gavel Award from Toastmaster's International.

///

I grew up in the greatness of the secret that Earl Nightingale shared with my dad. Some kids grow up watching cartoons. Some kids grow up playing with blocks. I grew up listening to Earl Nightingale and memorizing Marcus Garvey monologues. I had no idea that our family was different.

By the time I was five years old, my grandmother's floor-cleaning days were over. Her little boy, Leslie, had managed to find a worthy ideal. He had utilized the H.A.R.V.A.R.D. Effect to become the Earl Nightingale of the 80s. He would go on to produce his first set of motivational audio programs: *Getting Unstuck*, and *Keys to Self-Motivation*, *Power of a Larger Vision*, and *You Gotta Be Hungry*. These would be the lullabies that raised me.

Even though we did not live together at the time, I never felt separated from the family business. Before going out on one speaking tour, my assignment was to study the speakers who graced the stage a year before my father. After watching their full presentations, he would ask me to make suggestions and to outline their most impactful pointers. I had no idea at the time that I was being trained up to be a part of a motivational team that had never existed before.

By the time I was nine years old, my dad was a massive success in the human potential industry. I would watch how hard he worked to customize presentations for his corporate audiences. Those are still my warmest memories. All his success came from progressing toward one simple, yet worthy, ideal. That ideal was to buy Ms. Mamie Brown a home. That was the ideal that started my dad's awe-inspiring career. Little did he know that he would, eventually, buy my grandmother not just a home, but three different homes.

In just one generation, under Mamie Brown's leadership, she adopted and raised a son who would help the Brown family transition from cleaning other people's floors on Miami Beach to hiring housekeepers to come and clean her floors on Miami

Beach. Taking in the beautiful basketball court and Olympic-size swimming pool with a slide, I truly believed that my dad was a superhero. Even though he never went to college, he found a way to graduate to a level in life that I can only attribute to the

H.A.R.V.A.R.D. Effect.

Everything was perfect. I felt as happy as I imagine David Suderski felt when he received the key to his boat. But, then, our family was rocked by the worst thing that could happen. My grandmother, the wonderful woman who had devoted all the warmth in her heart to her family, was diagnosed with breast cancer.

On my tenth birthday—May 22, 1994—I found myself sitting down in the living room, trying to wrap my head around moving into the double digits of age. In a complete contrast to the usual hustle and bustle of family life, the house was still. Silent. The uncertainty was apparent.

All my grandmother's adopted children were in the house, and the sadness hung so heavy in the air that it felt smothering. Since I was so young, I didn't understand what had happened and was thinking more about my birthday than anything else. That is, until my father walked out of the room with tears in his eyes, something I had never seen before. He had held his beloved mother's hand as she took her last breath. That day, my tenth birthday, my grandmother had passed away.

As everybody wept, I wondered how we were going to get through this as a family unit. I wondered how my Dad was ever going to give a speech about her without breaking down. I wondered if it was some type of sign that she passed away on this day, and, if so, what did it mean?

Several days later, during my grandmother's funeral, the First Family of Motivation was born. The church was filled with people whose lives she had touched. Press clamored outside, trying to ask my dad questions. At the time, my dad was married to the legendary singer, Gladys Knight, and she sang a beautiful song in honor of my grandmother.

The truly remarkable turn of events was yet to come. During the service, the chaplain asked if anyone wanted to get up and share something from their heart about Mamie Brown. As I sat there, a young boy of just 10 years old, I felt compelled to share. This would be the first time that I had ever touched a microphone. This would be the first time that I would ever look at an audience from a platform and taste the expectations in the air. This would be the first time that I would open my heart and allow my words to latch onto somebody else's.

That day, I wasn't speaking to the audience. I was speaking to my grandmother. The only reaction that I remember was the look in my dad's eyes after the service when it was just the two of us. He told me that, one day, my voice would carry the family name to the next generation. He told me that I was gifted and that there was greatness in me.

Obviously shocked that I had the courage to share at such a young age, the following week, he asked if I would travel on the road with him and introduce him before he spoke at his engagements. I thought of how my grandma would feel and know that she would be proud, so I readily agreed. The next week, I was on tour with the top speaker in the world—my dad- and he became my professor and my biggest cheerleader as well as my coach.

Eventually, I was doing such a great job at introducing him that I was assigned different motivational monologs to memorize. My dad would randomly bring me up before audiences of thousands of people to test whether I had truly learned it. As the saying goes, "If you stay ready, you don't have to get ready." I didn't have to worry. When it came to representing the Brown dynasty on behalf of John Bryant and Mamie Brown, I was always ready.

The Coattails of Greatness

As a teenager, I started carrying the torch on behalf of my grandmother.

Now, at the age of 31, I had the opportunity to share our family story before Harvard graduates. When I got the news about this incredible opportunity I thought about two things:

1. I knew that even though Ms. Mamie Brown didn't travel often, this was an occasion that she would not have missed for the world. I wished that she could be there on that day to hear me speak from my heart. I wanted to make her proud.

2. I realized that I was not even close to being ready for the moment that was approaching.

I had given more than 2,000 professional speeches since the age of 10 years old. By the time I was 14, I started earning a nice living by working in the family business. My first offer for a paid speaking engagement was for $2,500. That would be the lowest paycheck that I would ever cash. I always remembered my dad reminding audiences, "You don't get paid by the hour, you get paid based on the value that you bring to the hour." I kept that lesson in my heart. Growing up in a family that always believed the impossible was possible turned me into an expert on success at an early age.

Even though I had given speeches internationally in front of thousands before, I knew I was not ready to present at Harvard. My best speech was still stuck inside of me. I was no longer a teenage boy speaking about success. It was time to put my Harvard speech together.

Success was the only option for me, but it also terrified me. Out of all my eleven siblings, I was the first one to venture into a career as an inspirational speaker. My oldest sister, Ona, would later overcome her shyness and join our father-son duo. We were labeled the First Family of Motivation during our debut international tour.

I never get nervous. I'm always ready to tackle a challenge. But, when Harvard called, I questioned myself. Can you imagine the pressure I felt to make sure the speech that I gave was better than any other speech I had given in my entire life? That is when I realized that I needed to apply the H.A.R.V.A.R.D Effect for myself.

The H.A.R.V.A.R.D. Effect is designed to give you all the tools you need to thrive in the opportunities that come your way. It forces you to question yourself. Have you ever had a desire deep within your heart to increase your performance? Maybe you've received a call from one of the Harvards of your industry? Or been offered an opportunity that required you to be better than you have ever been? This book focuses on the most relevant techniques that will help you to become better than you have ever been.

What you are about to read is like no other information product ever produced. Together, we are going to be walking through the step-by-step process that I had the privilege of sharing at Harvard University.

Earl Nightingale is no longer with us. The strangest secret in the world must be updated. Napoleon Hill and other inspiring figures—such as Jim Rohn, Myles Munroe, and Wayne Dyer—have left us. Now, it is time to continue with their great work, adapted for a modern world.

I don't want to tell you a bunch of fluff about how you can get rich, nor how you can implement better business strategies. I am not focusing my gifts on making people laugh, nor keeping them entertained. This is about the business of you.

Perhaps this book isn't for you. I believe that, out of the thousands of people who will apply to implement the H.A.R.V.A.R.D. Effect in their lives, only a small percentage will earn their rites of passage through these chapters that I share from my heart. This is an advanced curriculum. Many of the things that I may require you to take action on might not make sense to you immediately. If, at any time, you feel uncomfortable, feel free to drop out. But, if you are ready to take action, if you are ready to open yourself to success, this is the book you've been waiting for.

As I started planning this book, I thought back over all the things that I learned throughout my career and how I could insert only the most effective and relevant points into my guide for you. I began to think to myself that success isn't what it used to be. The version of success for this generation is much different. Therefore, the reality of what it truly means to be successful cannot remain stuck in time.

If Earl Nightingale was right—if success is the realization of a worthy ideal—I would say that people are ready for a new realization. The worthy ideals of the past will not cut it as we shift into the future. If you don't already have a worthy ideal for your life, please stop reading this book now. This is the

H.A.R.V.A.R.D. Effect. You are not truly prepared to enroll in this process if your ideals are worthy of world-class recognition.

I don't care about your SAT scores. I don't care whether you went to a private school or only got a third-grade education. I don't care what qualifications and experience you have. All you need to be qualified to walk on this campus of super-achievement is a worthy ideal. The world needs more people who are willing to bring their worthy ideals to life. Your life, itself, is a worthy ideal. Let us not question if we are ready for the unknown.

If you are ready to enter the Ivy League of personal development, keep reading. If you want to know what it truly takes to go beyond your own version of success, keep reading. I am a member of the First Family of Motivation. I was born to be a doubt assassin. By studying these strategies and applying them to your life, your confidence will become a lethal weapon.

If true greatness was a fluke, I would tell you. If massive achievement was some type of grand conspiracy, I would be your whistleblower. I wouldn't waste my time writing a book about high achievement if it was based in fiction. When I fasten my red tie in the locker room getting ready to step on the stage, I wonder if I'm going to have a Zig Ziglar moment. I ask infinite intelligence to bring out the best that I have to offer, because my father's footsteps are a worthy ideal to me.

The Sequence of Massive Achievement

Anyone can read a self-help book and go out and repeat what they read. I have learned that there are three curriculums of high achievement that you can achieve whether you went to Harvard, Yale, or, like me, Pasadena City Community College. When you experience these three curriculums of high achievement, you will discover the exhilarating process they entail.

The first curriculum is something I'm sure you are familiar with, something us gurus in self-help like to call the Dream Phase. This is an elementary school for high-achievers.

Think back to how easy and how free you felt while in elementary school. You didn't have a care in the world. Your only goal was to have fun. Your main agenda was to play with your friends and enjoy yourself. That is how it feels when you are in the dream phase.

Many times, your dream feels silly. Am I wrong for saying that? When you first realize your dream and haven't accomplished it yet, you begin to think about how you might feel if you *did* accomplish it. It makes you feel silly. I know you're familiar with the dream phase, but has your dream ever made you feel like a little kid again? Where just the thought brings a smile to your face?

If you are reading this, you know about the dream phase. Has your dream ever made you feel like a little kid again? Has the thought of it brought a smile to your face?

Contrary to what Facebook and many dating apps may believe, you are not the face that you see in the mirror. The body is composed of bone and cellular tissue. You are not your body. You *have* a body. But you are more than the vehicle that you use to live. Your body temple is what you *have*, but your dream temple is what you *are*.

Your dream phase represents the authentic data of your identity. Your dream says more about who you are than your name or even your DNA. I often wonder, when did they begin to label our highest ideas as dreams? We know what a dream is when a person is sleeping, but why did they start labeling our worthy ideas dreams?

In ancient times, before the days of the smartphone and HD television, a dream while a person slept was the most engaging form of entertainment. It was the grand cinema of life, one that every man and woman received a ticket to attend. Many civilizations, including the Greeks, considered the dream phase while sleeping to be a medium between our earthly world and the heavenly realm. This was before science used technology to study what happens in the brain while our heads rest on our pillows. Many years later, the philosopher Carl Jung taught modern society that the dreams we have while sleeping represent unresolved, repressed wishes.

Later down the line in history, curious minds who call themselves neuroscientists discovered the science of dreaming. They teach us that the dream phase of sleeping usually occurs in only one of the five stages of sleep. The fifth stage of sleep, also known as the REM stage, is a fascinating concept. It is during this stage that researchers learned about the rapid eye movement that takes place behind the closed lashes of a sleeper.

Every time I ever went to sleep, I didn't think about what stage of sleep I was in. I just thought sleep was sleep. So did the ancient Greeks. I had no idea about how our brains produce five different types of electrical waves, nor did I know that when we dream, the brain waves known as *theta* become more active. The *theta* wave is responsible for activating the part of the brain that generates mental imagery.

Now, we can examine why we call our worthy ideas dreams and why the dream phase while awake is so crucial for massive achievement. At Rome University, there was a breakthrough in sleep science while a research team was investigating something called dream recall. They wanted to study the reason why some people remember their dreams, while others don't. During their experiment, where they invited 65 students to spend two nights in their laboratory, and they connected their brains to an EEG machine. It was revealed that the neurophysiological mechanisms that we employ while dreaming—and recalling dreams—are the same as when we construct and retrieve memories while we are awake.

Dream Paralysis

Maybe the Greeks were right. Maybe Carl Jung wasn't wrong. The fact of the matter remains that they did not have access to the science of dreaming, like we do today. I am not a neuroscientist, nor a philosopher. I am a second-generation motivator. My job in this book is to share the science of a different type of dream. Not the ones you have when your eyes are closed, but the ones that you feel when your heart is open.

To truly analyze the dreams that I'm referring to, we must examine heart waves, instead of brainwaves. I think that the reason why we call our greatest ideas "dreams" is because, once we experience our dream phase, it can be hard for us to believe that it is truly reality.

When we bring our dreams to life and watch them appear in our earthly realm, we sometimes believe that it is some type of neurological illusion, thinking that our theta waves are playing tricks on us. Yes, the dreams that are inside you when you sleep and the dreams you have when you are awake are very different, but they have a lot more in common than most people realize.

There is a rare mental disorder called Charcot-Wilbrant Syndrome. In this syndrome, people can lose the functions of the brain and cease to dream during sleep hours. It is a type of mind blindness. Unfortunately, there are many people who suffer from this unnatural syndrome during their waking hours, as well.

My dad was speaking to a group in South Africa a short time ago. He gave a 60-minute presentation to a group of thousands who were seeing him on their continent for the first time. A land that Napoleon Hill and Earl Nightingale never set foot on. A land that, until recent years, had been oppressed. A land where the strangest secret in the world remains a secret.

He told them that they had the power to live their dreams. No matter how big it was, he saw, firsthand in his own life, how dreams can come true. When he finished, the crowd erupted in applause, as they usually do. (#MyDadIsAwesome)

But, after this speech, there was a question from the audience that he had never received in over 40 years as intellectual resource. One of the participants saw him after the speech and humbly asked, "Mr. Brown, thank you for traveling all the way to our country to teach us how to live our dreams. But, Mr. Brown, how do you dream?"

To dream while you are awake, it requires more than having your eyes open, just as it requires more to dream while you are asleep than for your eyes to be closed. We will not have the luxury that the dream phase in life provides us, unless we find ourselves in a REM state of awakening. REM is the only time we really dream while sleeping, and, if you are woken up during REM sleep, you are likely to recall your dreams. I have discovered that, in life, there is a REM state of being awake. This REM state stands for Repetitious Empowering Message.

When one hears a repetitious empowering message over and over, just as my dad listened to David Sidursky's record over and over, it stimulates the brain in your heart that enables dream capability. Some people suffer from mind blindness and are unable to dream while they are awake, because they have never been exposed to a repetitious, empowering message. So many messages that they are exposed to are negative and depressing. When they analyze the political landscape, the economy, or the news, it can be difficult to find inspiration that stimulates the "theta" waves of the heart into a mental image of a better future. *[handwritten: Come off the phone, social media, daily news!]*

Dreams while you are asleep are formed in the head, during the REM stage of sleeping. Dreams while you are awake are formed in the heart, during the REM stage of awakening. If you know of someone who doesn't truly know what their dream in life is, don't give them this book. This book is not for the elementary school achiever who has yet to enter a REM state. That is a different process than the one we will embark on in this book.

I have developed an audio series, *The High Hopes for Your Future*, which has several repetitious, empowering messages that would be more suitable for those who have yet to enter into—or who are still in—the dream phase.

Some people know what their dream is. They have heard repetitious, empowering messages and believed them. They stop looking at what is happening in their marketplace or in the news, and they get in tune with their "heartmath." Sometimes, it is hard to see how your greatness will add up to anything when you do the math in your head, but there is a new type of arithmetic that the HeartMath Institute has discovered, which has given way to a new discipline, known as neuroradiology.

In 1991—seven years after Ms. Mamie Brown passed away—Dr. J. Andrews Armour discovered that there is a sophisticated nervous system in the heart that qualifies as a 'little brain.' The little brain of the heart is composed of an elaborate network that is very similar to the brain in our heads. This is the place where dreams are born.

Remember, you are not your skin color, nor are you your social security number or your bank account. You are more than a bunch of cells wrapped in flesh.

When I became a father, I went to the doctor during the early stages of the pregnancy. I was shocked to learn that doctors determine whether a baby is healthy early on by monitoring the fetus's heart rate. Before we are born, the first thing that appears in a mother's womb is not a finger, nor a toe, nor a face. Not even a brain. When we first arrived on this earthly realm, what shows up first, is a heart. Your heart then sends the instructions that grow the rest of your body, including the brain.

We all start off as a heart. Not as an employee, nor a student. You are a heart. Your heart has a body. Even though you think your body has a heart, the heart was here first. Your *heart* has a *body*.

The heart is, therefore, the root of your existence. When you enter the dream phase of awakening, your heart will reveal your true purpose for living. Neurocardiology can tell you what the heart does; however, only *you* can demonstrate and understand the dream that your heart brain was born with. I believe that my job as a thought leader is to place you into a REM state while you are awake. That is why I am constantly working on repetitious empowering messages that will enable people to dream beyond what their eyes can see.

The dream phase is just the first curriculum of massive achievement. It is crucial, but is just the beginning. Far too many people suffer from dream paralysis.

Sleep paralysis is the feeling of being conscious, but unable to move. Dream paralysis is the feeling of having a dream that you are conscious of, but, for some reason, you are unable to act on it and pull it from your heart to this earthly realm. Do you know anyone who suffers from dream paralysis? People who like talking about what they would like to see in their lives, but rarely put in the work? People who have been held back in the elementary school of achievement and never make it to the secondary curriculum?

It is not enough to have a dream. That is the starting point. Although there is a quote that says, "A civilization is only as great as its dreams," the Dream Phase is not designed to be self-fulfilling. The awareness that a dream brings will unleash a momentum that can usher us from the dream phase into the destiny phase.

Dreaming is not enough. Your dreams tell you who you are, but far too many of us get stuck at that elementary level of achievement. Even if they do manage to get exposed to a repetitious, empowering message—or REM state-- while wake that causes them to become aware of what their dream for their life is, for some reason, they allow dream paralysis to take over, and they never act on their dreams.

Your dreams were not placed in your heart to remain there. The dreams that the little brain in your heart placed in you were to show you who you are, so that you can use the big brain in your head to show the planet what you can do. Your dream is about who. Your destiny is about what.

At Harvard University, they have mastered the art of teaching students how to properly use the big brain in the head. In the H.A.R.V.A.R.D. EFFECT, it will require you to flex the muscle of the little brain that is in your heart. When both brains collaborate in harmony, we graduate from elementary school and enter the high school of higher achievement. You were not born to pay bills. We were not created to be permanent consumers. You were born to turn the dreams of your heart into a destiny for yourself.

Just as it requires a higher than average IQ to get into Harvard University, it requires an even higher EQ to move from the dream phase to the destiny phase. In Daniel Goleman's *Emotional Intelligence*, he writes, "the pervading view of human intelligence as mind intellect is just too narrow of a view." He believes—and I agree—that, "It ignores a range of human capacities that bear equal if not greater weight in determining our successes in life." IQ stands for intelligence quotient.

Your dream is all about your capability. Your destiny is about your capacity. If you have a dream, it is very important that you develop the capacity to graduate into a destiny. What I like to consider the high school of high achievement. People who are no longer satisfied with dreaming. When they have a dream, they take action and do whatever is required to live their dreams while they are awake. They already know who they are. They are no longer questioning what they are here for. Instead, they are always busy executing the necessary habits and attitudes that are required to carve out a destiny.

When you turn your dream into an experience, you will arrive at the destiny phase. We read about people in this phase all the time. The incredible potential that turns into earning power. I remember the joy that I once had while traveling around with my father and lighting crowds on fire with the set pieces that he had me memorize.

It was one of my dreams to follow in my father's footsteps. The opportunity to give a speech at Harvard University, nearly 21 years later, was part of my destiny. The sense of fulfillment I had when I took the microphone and began to share the H.A.R.V.A.R.D. Effect at Harvard University before the graduate students and members of the student government. That was way more than a dream. It was a destiny moment.

Many people think that my gift as a public speaker was some type of natural talent. That somehow my dad's genetic imprint on me helped to cultivate my unique speaking tool. Maya Angelou has a quote that I love. When people asked if she was a natural poet, she said, "Show me a natural brain surgeon, and I'll show you a natural poet." She meant that it takes a lot of work to be at the top of your field. I have been putting in a lot of work over the years, but I have yet to reach celebrity status. Many people know my dad, however, and my following is just now beginning to grow. It meant so much to me that I had gone beyond one of my dreams by making that dream of mine to speak at the most prestigious campus on the planet a part of my destiny.

One time, my hero, I mean my dad, got invited to the private home of one of the most powerful female voices who ever walked the face of this earth. She, too, knew about the H.A.R.V.A.R.D. effect. Her name was Ms. Maya Angelou. When he told me about this experience, I asked how it happened and why he didn't take me with him. He told me that David, one of his speaker coaching clients who was in his early 20s, had arranged it. I knew David. We were around the same age.

Now I really got curious. Not only did he go and meet with the 'Empress of Poetry' and the 'Oracle of

Global Empowerment' without me, he went there with David.

I said, "Dad, please explain, I need more details." He said, "One of David's lifelong dreams was to meet Maya Angelou. He somehow found the contact information for

Maya Angelou's office and called them." I was shocked.

Like David, I, too, have a great deal of love and respect for Maya Angelou. It had been one of my lifelong dreams to be able to meet her, too, but David turned it into his destiny.

I had one final question to ask of my father, even though a thousand more were circulating through my mind. I said, "What did David say when he got in contact with Ms. Maya Angelou's office? He smiled as he slid the dagger of truth through my little heart brain's dream. "He said, 'Hi, my name is David, and I'm calling on behalf of Mr. Les Brown. It has been one of Mr. Brown's lifelong dreams to meet Ms. Maya Angelou. Do you think that that can be arranged?'"

Wow! I couldn't help but laugh. Ms. Maya Angelou's team said, "Yes, she would love that." David called my dad and asked if he could set up a meeting between the two of them, and my Dad agreed, inviting David to go along with him.

I was so mad at David. I wish I could tell you that I was proud of him. The fact is that I can clearly remember how it felt to hear that he was willing to put in the work. When I looked at David and sized him up as a human being, I didn't think David had that in him. No offense, David, if you're reading this.

I didn't know he had that high of an EQ. It wasn't a high IQ that made his dream come true; it was his EQ. I could have easily called the office myself and asked if there could be a meeting between one of the most inspirational female voices on the planet and one of the most transformational male voices on the planet. That didn't require a graduate degree from Harvard or Morehouse. It required a high EQ.

David knew about the H.A.R.V.A.R.D. effect.

The Emotional Genius

According to Wikipedia, "Emotional intelligence or emotional quotient (EQ) is the capability of individuals to recognize their own, and other people's emotions, to discriminate between different feelings and label them appropriately, and to use emotional information to guide thinking and behavior." Now, if you have a low EQ and you have a dream, but have yet to graduate to the destiny phase, this book isn't for you. If you don't know what it feels like to go from underdog to top dog, you probably are not ready for the next seven chapters. In fact, the first letter in the effect might stop you in your tracks. Stop reading this book now.

Don't worry. I have put together a powerful audio series, *Claim Your Destiny*, which is custom-made to help people graduate from the dream phase to the destiny phase.

Destiny is not a result of fate, nor of cosmic configuration. Destiny is a decision. When the dreams in your heart begin to synchronize with the power of your mind, destiny arrives. To bring your dreams to life, you must take an EQ test called destiny. You will fully understand what I mean when we look at the purpose and origins of the IQ test.

In 1883, Jean-Martin Charcot (who the Charcot-Wlibrandt syndrome is named after) hired and mentored a young man named Alfred Binet to work in his neurological laboratory. According to Carol S. Dweck's *Mindset*, Alfred Binet—who went on to become the inventor of the IQ test—did not do so to summarize children's unchangeable intelligence. Carol Dweck wrote, "Binet, a Frenchman working in Paris in the eighteenth century. Designed the test to identify the students who were not profiting from the Paris public schools, so that new educational programs could be designed to get them back on track. He believed that education and practice could bring about fundamental changes in intelligence."

I think Alfred Binet was as right as my mother was when she told Les Brown early in his career that he had gold in his mouth. Your destiny will require a fundamental change in both your mental and emotional intelligence. Your heart and your head both have brains inside of them. Many universities focus solely on your IQ. Mental genius is welcome at all universities, because, back in the day, mental intelligence was the driving force for competitive advantage.

Just because you have book smarts does not mean that you have the emotional literacy that is necessary to thrive in the destiny phase. We see many people rise to the top with talent and, then, plummet to the bottom. Their dream was only a temporary phase, because the power of their heart never synchronized with the greatness of their minds.

Your destiny is the ultimate balance. Hopefully, you have graduated from Destiny High. This effect that you are about to enroll in is fully equipped with the necessary ingredients to give you much more than a competitive advantage.

There is a concept called Buffet-ology—named after Warren Buffet—that reveals how he was able to dream of wealth into a destiny of abundance. While most investors would sell their equity in their investments after a certain amount of return was achieved, young Warren decided to do a little more research and maintain ownership in organizations that have what he calls "a durable competitive advantage," with "future growth opportunities."

Nowadays, a temporary competitive advantage is not enough. That brings us to the topic at hand. The third curriculum, High Achievement. That is something called the Dynasty Phase. After the dream phase comes the destiny phase. I hope you have graduated from both.

Now, let me welcome you to the higher learning of high achievement. You will be required to use your IQ, your EQ, and any other Q you can possibly think of to fully graduate with honors from the H.A.R.V.A.R.D. EFFECT.

The opportunity to speak on that beautiful campus was not just something for me to put on my resume. For me, it was an opportunity to make a difference in the lives of the next generation of trailblazers. I figured that graduate students at an Ivy League college would probably already know about the dream phase. It takes a lot of repetitious empowering messages to get into a top university. Especially with all the modern distractions that many of our young people must deal with. Many people out there can give you some great tips about the destiny phase, as well. What it takes to make it through tough times. How to handle rejection and setbacks. There are a ton of powerful motivators on the issue of what to do to reach your destiny. The dream is about who. Destiny is about what. Your Dynasty is about why.

When the faculty at Harvard University asked me what topic I was going to speak on, I knew what it was. The topic was going to be something very different and powerful. The name of the event was called "Success, The Only Choice." My speech was going to be titled "Position Your Dynasty."

You are a walking breathing Dynasty. That is why you are reading this book. We are in the process of carving out a durable competitive advantage for ourselves. I think that success means something totally different for my generation than it did for my grandmother and father's generations. I believe that we live in a time wherein even success is not good enough. It is important to be able to update and refine and reboot our definitions of success. This book is for people who, like Harvard University students, already know that success is the only choice.

There are different degrees of success. The strategies in this book will equip you in what I consider a doctorate degree in self-improvement.

I have been involved in the human potential industry for over 21 years. This industry annually generates over $65 billion worldwide. My family and I had a dream to climb to the top of that food chain, and we turned it into our destiny. Dynasty is a succession of people from the same family who play a prominent role in business, politics, or another field.

What is the point of becoming a high achiever, if you can't share it with your family? Not just the fruits, but also the roots. When one of the top insurance companies in the world interviewed the wealthiest families, they asked what the main things they wanted to leave behind for their children were. The answer had nothing to do with their fortunes. They said they wanted to leave behind their stories and their values.

Like my speech at Harvard, this book is jam-packed with the stories and values that have inspired me to make a greater difference in the world. When you become an alumni of the H.A.R.V.A.R.D. EFFECT, you will, essentially, be joining the First Family of Motivation. I want you to use this curriculum to go out and make a difference in your marketplace.

Use everything that I share with you to go out and position your dynasty. Play a prominent role on the planet. The dynasty phase is not all about you. If you are still stuck there, go back to the dream phase. Once one has a destiny, one realizes the importance of paying it forward. You will be graded in this course not by what you do for yourself, but, instead, by how you use these strategies to play a prominent role in giving back to others.

Immortal Impact

Many people never make it to the dynasty phase of achievement. I have often wondered why the people who seem to give the most always find a way to earn the most. I believe that there is a way to become immune to death. There is a level of achievement that I call the dynasty phase, wherein one lives their lives and they die, yet they still have future growth opportunities from beyond the grave.

It's hard for me to stomach the thought of mortality. I remember getting a call from my dad in my early teenage years while I was in Valencia, California, about to go to a school basketball game. I answered the phone, and he said, "Hello, Great One, how are you?" I said, "Rich and happy, Dad. How are you today?" He told me he'd had better days, and I instantly knew that something was wrong.

My dad's usual saying was "I'm better than good and better than most and, sometimes, even better than that." I heard something in his voice that I had not heard since my grandmother had passed away.

He asked me if I was sitting down and told me, "I was doing my radio show in New York, and the topic was prostate cancer. My guest was encouraging our listeners to get their prostate exam done." He went on to explain, "That show inspired me to get tested. I just left the doctor's office, and they told me that I have prostate cancer and

might only have a few years left to live."

"Cancer, Dad? What does that mean?"

He said, "I don't know right now. I just wanted to tell you the news." We hung up. I was too shocked to cry. Some say the word "cancer" is the most feared word in every language. I thought about how much I loved my father. I wasn't ready to lose my hero. I was just 13. If he had listened to what the doctors said, my father would have died, fully knowing about the dream phase and even the destiny phase. However, because of his EQ, he kicked cancer's butt, and he earned an opportunity to witness his Dynasty phase come full circle. Even after he and I are both gone, this curriculum will be making a long-term difference in the world.

Dad, I love you. Thank you for positioning our dynasty. Thank you for making the tough choices in how you eat and exercise, so, at the age of 71, you can hold your grandson, Honor Phoenix Brown. Thank you for being there for me in the front row at Harvard University. Thank you for teaching me about the H.A.R.V.A.R.D. effect.

Did you know that the person who Harvard University is named after was a man who died at the early age of 31? New College or the College at New Towne was established over one hundred years before the American Revolution in 1636. Three years later, the son of a butcher whose family had been mostly wiped out by the plague died from tuberculosis. His name was John Harvard. He had no children, but, in his will, he ordered that 700 euros and nearly 400 books be donated to the New College. Shortly after, they officially changed their name.

John Harvard died at the same age I am as I write this book. However, he had no idea that his dynasty would have future growth opportunities beyond his lifespan. This young man has made an immortal impact on history. So will you, once you position your dynasty.

As we conclude this orientation, there is one assignment all H.A.R.V.A.R.D. effect scholars must complete before moving forward on this campus of possibility. It requires you to memorize a motivational monolog that all Harvard University students and faculty use as a repetitious empowering message to ensure that the dream of Harvard became a destiny. And we all know, Harvard University has something more than a destiny. It has the largest endowment and is currently worth over $37 billion. Among its alumni are six U.S. presidents and 21 Nobel Prize winners. That's what I call a dynasty.

This effect will enable you to position your dynasty. Before we get started, I want you to take the time and memorize this REM, the Harvard Creed. You don't need to be a Harvard graduate to learn its creed. How empowering would it be for your children or your co-workers if they knew about the Harvard creed? If you want to gain the strength of the philosophy in the chapters to come, do not skip this first step, learning the same creed that made John Harvard an immortal icon in education.

Commit the Harvard Creed to memory, as though it is the Pledge of Allegiance. Once you have this memorized, your orientation is complete, and you can begin your freshman course in the H.A.R.V.A.R.D. EFFECT.

I AM HARVARD

All men know my fame and outward aspect. But my sons alone know my heart.

Not from narrow confines do my sons come to me. They make their way from the East, where I have grown from small beginnings nearly three centuries ago, side by side with the growth of a great nation and as an integral part of its faith and striving. They make their way from the West, where vigorous American manhood, with its face to the setting sun, hewed out an empire and established the fighting spirit of truth throughout a great land. They come to me from the

South and the North, from every farm and village and city, where clean hearted, cleareyed boys have turned toward me as the mother of colleges, the great teacher of opportunities grasped and dreams come true.

They are the builders who have made me great. And on what foundation stones, think you, have they built? On money? On family tradition? They have wrought with materials more eternal.

They have laid my foundations on faith, on eternal visions of fair dealing, and fashioned my greatness with red-blooded manhood and shoulder to shoulder contact with their fellow men.

Where the call of conflict is there will my sons be found. Where victories are won my sons will be triumphant. And where great causes for a time go crashing to defeat my sons will take their medicine like men. But the truth that burns in their hearts can never die.

Because the war was fought for right I gave unsparingly of my sons and my resources. And not until the last great battle of freedom and justice is fought shall my task be complete. I ask no man for money. I do my work with my eyes upon the eternal stars and my feet upon the grim realities of American life and the problems and dreams of its vital and human men and women.

But as truth will endure, so shall the vision in the sons of Harvard endure.

As they are strong, so shall I be strong.

For I am Harvard, the mother of colleges, the home of truth, the dwelling place of men.

Harvard will see it through!

I agree with the Harvard Creed. The truth that burns in your heart can never die. In my opinion, that is what every child in America should be learning. Your dynasty will be wrought with eternal materials. The word "wrought" means beaten out or shaped by hammering. That sexy word "eternal" is an adjective which means lasting or existing forever; without end or beginning.

You can't position your dynasty by dreaming about it. It is easy to get stuck in the high school of destiny by getting too busy to consider your immortal impact, which is your dynasty. The reason most people never build a dynasty is because it requires more than positive thoughts. A dynasty requires more than a vision board or an inheritance. A dynasty must be shaped by hammering. We must find a way to shape our dynasties, so that we live out the truth in our heart, allowing the best parts of us to live forever.

Your dream is about *who*. Your destiny is about *what*. Your dynasty is about *why*.

The first step in the effect is, perhaps, the most difficult. If you don't have the discipline to memorize the Harvard Creed, you won't have the attention span to complete your freshman project.

Make a video of yourself repeating the Creed, and upload it to the members-only section of www.harvardeffect.com, or in our private Facebook group.

Handwritten:

The truth that lives in my heart can never die.
My dynasty will be wrought with eternal materials.
A Dynasty requires more than a vision board or an inheritance.
A dynasty must be shaped by hammering. We must find a way to shape our dynasties, so that we live out the truth in our heart, allowing the best parts of us to live forever.

Freshman Chapter

HUNDRED-YEAR PLAN

*"Live as if you were to die tomorrow.
Learn as if you were to live forever"*

-Mahatma Gandhi

Many millennials are more fascinated with pop culture than personal growth. I was exposed to both. The kid who knows all the greatest movies and artists of our time is rarely exposed to the intellectual pop stars who are part of my family's beloved industry. Brian Tracy, known as the global authority on time management, was just as engaging for me as a Britney Spears concert was to my peers.

Sometime after I got my own apartment in Atlanta, Georgia, I began alternating between days of listening to Brian Tracy and days of listening to Tupac Shakur, the Earl Nightingale of the hip-hop world.

As a teen, the hip-hop world caught my attention. There was only one conflict. Personal growth was teaching me about the curriculums of high achievement; whereas, pop culture was teaching me about hopelessness.

I would sit by myself and analyze the contrasting messages. Brian would say, "The key to success is to focus our conscious mind on the things we desire, not things we fear." While Tupac would say "I smoke to keep the pain out/ and if I wasn't high, I'd probably try to blow my brains out." Mr. Tracy wrote, "Leaders think and talk about the solutions, followers think and talk about the problems;" whereas, Mr. Shakur would write, "…givin' up cash/ to the leaders, knowin' damn well it ain't gonna feed us."

I was too shocked to stop listening. I didn't want to spend so much time studying leadership programs, only to turn into a leader who guides people towards an empty table. When I say feed people, I'm not talking about putting food on the table. I mean giving their minds some real substance to chew on. Tupac Shakur fatally passed away in 1996, at the age of 25, but, even a decade after his death, he released new music that would influence a whole generation of fans, selling over 70 million albums to people that he would never get a chance to meet.

One day, while preparing a speech I was to present to a national association of judges, a fresh idea came to me. That evening in the banquet hall, I said a quote that I would later become known for in my career. They didn't have the handheld mic style I prefer, so I was forced to stand behind a podium. I mustered up the courage to say it for the first time. "If you can turn on the radio and learn how to be a thug, you should be able to turn on the radio and learn how to be a thinker." The crowd responded in applause, and I knew that I wasn't the only one who felt that way.

Imagine if pop culture and personal development collided with each other. Imagine if the lessons that were taught in seminars were as popular as some of the nonsense that is taught at concerts.

At the age of 19, my silver-spoon lifestyle took a drastic change. I decided to master a skill I thought would make my impact an immortal one. Although I was already the highest paid teen speaker in America, I was willing to give it all up, to become a positive hip-hop artist.

My goal was to study the messages in self-help and put them in a form that would inspire a whole new generation of achievers. Needless to say, my father was not very excited to hear the news. I went from being the golden boy to the black sheep of the family, nearly overnight. I was just beginning my dream phase, and all my father's wisdom could not shelter me from my untested ignorance about the power of dynasty.

For five years, I worked on my newfound love of creating motivational hip-hop music. During that time, I rarely spoke to my hero. It was clear that I had let him down.

I utilized everything I learned from the personal growth industry to turn my teenage dream ager into my Emmy Award-winning destiny in my early twenties. One of the people who really launched my career was a woman named Leila Steinberg. I saw a documentary Ms. Steinberg had put in theaters about Tupac Shakur. She started a workshop in the Bay Area that Tupac attended as a teenager. Leila had a father who was an attorney, and she would go to court with him as a child. She witnessed firsthand how justice can be manipulated to benefit the affluent. It was there that Leila began to consider what her calling could be. Leila believes that if artists were to use their voice for good, the world would be a better place. Her whole dynasty has been based on the concept of transforming artists into world-class leaders.

If Tupac Shakur had graduated from Harvard University, it is very likely that he would still be alive. But because he and Leila were well versed in the H.A.R.V.A.R.D. Effect, the truth that burned in his heart will live forever. Tupac Shakur watched his mother get stuck in the dream phase. He watched as she went from speaking at Harvard University to struggling to pay the bills and getting addicted to crack. It was apparent that he knew the wisdom of Brian Tracy, too, in his song "Dear Mama," which includes the lyrics, "And even as a crack fiend, Mama/ You always was a black queen, Mama." To this day, that song is the most motivational song for mothers that has ever been made. He clearly knew how to be a leader who thought about solutions.

Before Tupac was immortalized by his poetry, he slept on Leila's couch while his mom was overcoming dream abuse. Excuse me, I mean drug abuse. Attending her weekly workshop and developing his voice with a talented group of artists that included Leila and Ray Luv—a powerful lyricist who just happened to be Cab Calloway's grandson—among others. Leila would schedule shows for Tupac and Ray Luv. She helped them record his first album, which, eventually, earned them a multi-million-dollar recording career.

As Tupac's career was taking off, her father, the attorney, begged Leila to stop working in the hip-hop industry with Tupac. He offered to pay her to go and study under a man named Les Brown. He thought that his articulate daughter with a heart to serve would make a great motivational speaker. Leila told her father that she was not interested in working with him, because she was working with a voice that was going to change the music industry forever.

Her father's concern about the messages in hip-hop culture and its affinity for violence were not unjustified. At least 29 well-known hip-hop artists have suffered violent crimes in the past 20 years. Zero motivational speakers have shared the same fate. Like me, Leila wanted to use music as a form of medicine to help people cope with the grim realities of American life. When her friend and business partner was suddenly a victim of homicide, the destiny that she hustled so hard to build began to crumble. She would not work in the music industry for another ten years.

When I entered her class as a 22-year-old with short dreadlocks that were just beginning to blow in the wind, she was surprised to hear my story. I said, "I saw your documentary, *Tupac Resurrection*, in the theaters, and I heard you talk about turning artists into world leaders. I just want you to know that I'm the one."

She asked me who I was, and I told her my artist name was H.I.G.H. H.O.P.E.S., which stands for: Hip-Hop Intellectual Growing Higher Helping Other People Everywhere Soar. I told her that I had been a motivational speaker, but that, now, I wanted to put those same concepts into a form that could empower the next generation. She said her dad always wanted her to be a motivational speaker. When I revealed to her that I was Les Brown's baby boy, she was astonished by the coincidence.

It was during one of Leila's workshops that my dad and I reunited. Shortly after a senator from Harvard would become the President of The United States, I invited him to come and see me present at Leila's artist development workshop. The same one Tupac once attended. After my performance, Leila told my father that Tupac was the diagnosis. H.I.G.H. H.O.P.E.S. can be the antidote. I turned one of my father's old-school quotes into a catchy chorus. In the three 16-bar verses, I laid out the content that I usually had 30 to 60 minutes to cover in a keynote speech. The name of the song I performed was "I'll Never Be Broke Again." I remember hearing my dad have an audience of 30,000 women saying that over and over at a T.D. Jakes conference. Before a jam-packed house of the head law professor at USC private

Baldwin Hills Estate, I rocked the house! This moment would bring us back together. The beat came on, and I said:

> I'll Never be broke again,
> I'll Never be broke again.
> Not another day.
>
> 'I'll Never be broke again,
> I'll Never be broke again.
> Not in another way.
>
> I'll Never be broke again,
> I'll Never be broke again.
> Let me hear you say,
>
> I'll never be broke again,
> I'll never be broke again.

> I've been there, done that, and got the t-shirt.
>
> The size was too small, and the design needed some work.
> You can feel me if your paycheck don't match your worth.
> You can feel me if you only got pennies in your purse.
> And we cannot live our entire lives mad,
> Feeling limited because of a price tag
> You don't have to have the funds to deserve it,
> And if I don't have the ones, it doesn't mean that I'm not worth it.
> But you can't take that to the bank.
> So, I'll build my wealth, until I can take it take it to the bank.
> Because you're only welcome without a thanks
> When your mind is rich and your pockets ain't.

After the performance, my dad got up, and, in tears, told me that my voice was special. He told me that I was more than just an entertainer and reminded me that, now, I could speak the language of our youth, but I still had a dynasty to build in the human potential industry. Four words changed my destiny forever; "You can do both."

The following week I was back on tour with my Dad and sister Ona.

After the first speaking engagement that I'd had in quite a while, we all sat in a quaint little diner, discussing the future. It was there that I learned the strategy for the freshman assignment of the H.A.R.V.A.R.D. Effect.

Unlocking the Gates of Capacity

Redemption. I survived my dream and elevated to my destiny. Now, I was speaking and performing a song at the end. As I heard a story from my father for the first time, I knew the lesson of the story was just for me. While I was away in hip-hop land, working with the great Leila Steinberg, my father was traveling the world and working with the Gates family. After one of his speeches, they escorted him to a private room. A member of the Gates's inner circle said, "We heard you talk about your ten and twenty year goals, but we want to show you something." They pulled up a screen and said, "This is where the Gates Family will be in technology one hundred years from now."

When I heard this, I was baffled. I knew that Bill Gates was a Harvard dropout who founded one of the most profitable software companies in the world, but I had never heard of anyone thinking that far ahead. While at that diner, I realized that the Brown family, too, needed to formulate a hundred-year plan. I wanted to be the one to make it.

If you are already at the top of your industry, what does it take to permanently stay there? The co-director of Advanced Virtual and Technological Architectural Research (AVATAR), Dr. Rachel Armstrong, said, "When it comes down to a really positive future for humanity, the creativity that we possess, when the mind becomes embodied in the process of problem solving, is the most powerful technology that we have." At AVATAR, her job is to construct new ways of creating living architecture in space.

She has coined a term known as black-sky thinking. There is straight-line thinking, which is very logical and analytical. Practicality is the highest virtue for straight-line thinkers. Do you know of any straight-line thinkers in your family or workplace?

Straight-line thinking also has a cousin, named blue-sky thinking.

According to Dictionary.com, blue-sky thinking is creative thinking that is unfettered by convention. It means looking at the blue sky, without any clouds to block the vision.

Black-sky thinking is what you will be learning all about as a freshman, so that you can position your dynasty and implement the H.A.R.V.A.R.D. Effect. Here is a definition that I think sets the standard:

> "Black sky" is a term that refers to ventures into the unknown, implying existence at the edge of possibility. Black-sky thinking is a method for producing new kinds of future that enable us to move into uncharted realms with creative confidence.

Bill Gates is a black-sky thinker. That is the only possible explanation for his hundred-year plan. As I thought about the main message I wanted to convey while speaking at Harvard, this concept was the cornerstone. Many influential leaders from my industry encourage people to have a plan for their lives. Some urge audiences and readers to write down a one-year plan, or, maybe, a five-year plan. Why on earth would anyone need a hundred-year plan? You only need a hundred-year plan if you have a dynasty inside you.

As I began to think about a hundred-year plan for the Brown family, I started to move from blue-sky thinking to black-sky thinking. I knew that I wanted to make a hundred-year plan. After all, if it was good enough for the Gates family, it is good enough for mine—and yours, too. Here were some of the questions that I wanted answered: *How long does it take to make a hundred-year plan? What should it consist of? Where should it reside?*

That led me discover what would become the main takeaway I imparted on those bright students in Boston, which is also the main takeaway that I want to share with you during this semester. In the world of get-rich-quick schemes and think-positive overload, I have discovered the latest strangest secret in the world of business. I would like for us to access the same power of that secret in our personal lives.

This is a risky topic in a world in which many people are living month-to-month. They think in a straight line. How can you tell someone to make a century-long plan, when there are fewer than 100,000 people out of 7 billion total on the planet that ever live to be 100 years old? It almost seems like it would be a waste of time.

The difference between a century-long plan and a 21-day plan is not length, rather, it is language. When you make a plan that is all about you, it is okay to be short-sighted. Eventually, we end up losing all that we plan for, anyway. My childhood teacher, Marva Collins, once said, "I've never seen a U-HAUL truck, following a hearse." However, when you make a plan that is all about serving others, black-sky thinking is necessary.

A plan is an internal articulation that has eternal consequences. Short-term goals are very effective for dreamers, or people who are entering their destiny phase.

Short-term plans allow you to communicate with the past. But, after that, there is another level.

We all have short-term goals, whether it is for losing weight, earning more money, or to just to get to work on time. But they are often half-hearted, and, many times, people either don't complete them, or they resort to their old ways.

The reason for this is quite simple. A short-term plan is the language we use in the present to get away from our past. A long-term plan is the language we use to network with our future. When you make a plan with others, it requires outer speech.

Psychologists call the voice we use while talking to ourselves "inner speech." Inner speech is responsible for all planning. Little did we know in the days of Earl Nightingale and Napoleon Hill that the frontal lobe of the brain is active in the same way in both outer speech and inner speech.

Therefore, when you use your inner speech to plan, you are literally using a secret language that only you can speak. When you speak to yourself about short-term goals using your inner speech, you are doing so based on your present experience. How most of us view the world is a result of our experiences. Subsequently, I believe that short-term planning is a language that we use in the present to escape our past.

As we use inner speech to create a long-term plan, we are forced to consider the edge of possibility. I think that's why Bill Gates, while a student at Harvard, called a company and offered to sell a new software language to a computer company before the software was developed. He had classes to attend. He had not graduated from Harvard. Technically, he should have been tending to his schoolwork.

If he had graduated from Harvard, he could have been hired at a great job in any industry. Computers were not the multi-zillion dollar industry that it is today. While a freshman and sophomore at Harvard, he considered becoming a lawyer, like his father. Yet, the inner voice of his long-term plan guided him to make that call. The computer company was interested in the computer language he was selling, before the young Bill Gates even started to make it.

In his commencement speech, the leader of the computer revolution said,

> "What I remember above all about Harvard, was being in the midst of so much energy and intelligence. It could be exhilarating, intimidating, sometimes even discouraging, but always challenging. It was an amazing privilege. And, though I left early, I was transformed by my years at Harvard. The friendships I made and the ideas that I worked on. But taking a serious look back, I really have one big regret."

As I watched the YouTube video, I began to listen close, thinking to myself, *What regret does a man who is worth over $37 billion have?*

He continued,

> "I left Harvard with no real awareness of the awful inequities in the world. The appalling disparities of health and wealth and opportunity that condemn millions of people to lives of despair. I learned a lot here at Harvard about economics and politics. I got great exposure to the advances being made in the sciences. But humanity's greatest advancements are not in its discoveries, but how those discoveries are applied to reduce inequity. Whether through democracy, strong public education, quality health care or broad economic opportunity,

reducing inequity is the highest human achievement."

But, what if you only live to be 31, like John Harvard? Or 25, like Tupac Shakur? Do you still need a hundred-year plan? Your body is mortal. Your hundred-year plan represents the burning truth in your heart that will live forever. The main difference between a short-term plan and a hundred-year plan are the questions that we must ask ourselves to actualize them.

A short-term planner asks herself, *What do I really want to get out of life?* Why would a dynasty-focused individual set the bar so low? After all, none of what you get out of life can be taken with you. Many of us have already collected most of the things that we want for ourselves. To plan a hundred years ahead, it is going to take a philanthropic shift in the questions you ask.

Before I could answer what my hundred-year plan would be for the Brown family, I had to ask myself, "What unique value do I have to give to future generations?" Instead of asking what I need to have for myself while I am alive, black-sky thinkers must ask "How will the world be different because I was born?"

A plan is a form of intangible language that the universe can hear. The longer your plan is, the louder it gets, allowing the burning truth of your heart to be heard. Part of my hundred-year plan was to do both. For me to develop my skillset as an artist without abandoning my mindset as an intellectual resource.

Somehow, smaller parts of my hundred-year plan began to come true. On the flyer they used to promote the event, they placed my name and picture. It read, *John-Leslie Brown, Motivational speaker and Hip-Hop artist*. I was beyond excited — my dream of doing both had become my destiny.

The day of the engagement, I received a call from the world's leading motivational force. It was Mamie Brown's baby boy. He asked me what I would be speaking about. I didn't want all my talk about hundred-year plans to scare him. He said, "Son, just talk about your music. It says so much about who you are." He forgot something. I can do both.

In the article "Beyond Information Power," by Jamie McKenzie, he writes, "When we raise young people to cut and paste the best thinking of their elders, we shortchange them. New thinkers should amplify and improve upon the insights of their sages, heeding wisdom that has survived the tests of time and the vagaries of fashion."

During the 80s and 90s, my family taught about the dream and destiny phase of achievement. My goal was to improve on those insights. Not repeat them. I needed a new message. I finally formed the speech that was inside me. I just wasn't sure how it would be received.

As a teenager, I was punished for not writing a book. Just as I was instructed to memorize motivational monologues, I was asked to write a book. I didn't write one because I didn't want to be a cut-and-paste type of leader. Until I truly found a strategy that was unique and valuable, I would rather deal with being grounded than make money off something that wasn't truly groundbreaking. That is how I thought as a child. In the book *Live Your Dreams*, Les Brown noted, "Everybody's born unique, but most of us die copies." I knew I had finally found a message that I know will distinguish me from just being Les Brown's son.

I got on Periscope and asked people what the purpose of writing a book is. Some people said it is because it's your product. That answer repulses me. According to Google, there have been nearly 130,000,000 books written and published since the beginning of time. The reason I am writing this book is because it is part of my hundred-year plan. This tool is designed to empower high-achievers to be able to make an impact that lives beyond themselves. Even as a kid, I knew that my book would not be a product. My book will be more than a profit center. My goal for *The H.A.R.V.A.R.D. Effect* is that it be a pathway to reduced inequity.

My hundred-year plan consists of reducing the inequities for extraordinary people who may never have attended an extraordinary college. Too many of us think that, because we didn't go to an Ivy League college, we are not worthy of an Ivy League lifestyle. Will you partner with me to reduce the inequities of the future?

Your first assignment is to use your inner voice to create a hundred-year plan. This plan must be all about giving back. The only way to cure mortality is by reducing inequity in the future. Your dynasty is your immortal impact, and the foundation of that dynasty is your freshman assignment, your hundred-year plan.

Travelator Pitch

I know what you may be thinking. "I'm too busy to make a hundred-year plan." Chances are, you are not as busy as Bill Gates. You'd be happy to learn that I have found an exciting process that you can use to create this. In the past, businesses were typically the only entities that would plan that far into the future.

In his article, "100 Year Business Plans," Brian Gongol wrote,

> "The British foundry that cast Big Ben and the Liberty Bell has been in business consistently since 1570. To stay in business that long requires either a profound competitive advantage in some perpetually-in-demand product, or a remarkable capacity to adapt to the changing demands of the marketplace."

He went on to say,

> "The point of an ultra-long-term plan isn't to create a fixed, perfect roadmap for the next hundred years. Instead, the point is to pull management and ownership out of a fixation on quarterly results and into a view that asks what really ensures the company's purpose and existence as a going concern."

Your hundred-year plan outlines the highest version of your going concern. It is not to create a fixed result. As you produce your hundred-year plan, you will become a black-sky thinker who can adapt to the change and demands in life and death.

We were put on this planet to live, work hard, have fun, and die. There is a special part of each of us that deserves to be left behind. That aspect of our being that the world can't live without. Your hundred-year plan is your blueprint that will become the place where you inject all the burning truth in your heart. Let me teach you how to make a hundred-year plan in a way that is fun and fast.

The good news is that it does not take 99 years of life to make a hundred-year plan. You can make a hundred-year plan as early as 13 years old, the same age Bill Gates was when his middle school first got something called a computer.

The bad news is, it is going to require you to utilize a new mental software. A hundred-year plans sounds like a big task, but what does it look like? The first version of this assignment requires both a short inner speech and a short outer speech.

When I thought about how I would teach students to make a hundred-year plan, I realized the hardest part about having a plan of that size is answering the question, *Where should we put it? Should a plan with so much value be placed on paper which can be torn and lost? Should a plan that outlines the summary of your dynasty be stored on the Cloud somewhere, where any trained hacker can remove it?*

After an event in Phoenix, Arizona for the world's leading entrepreneurship organization, CEO Space, a member of the audience asked me to speak in private. I agreed. He said, "You were telling us to write down the ideas that are in our heads, but the only things we remember when we wake up in the morning are the ideas that we write in our hearts."

As a freshman in this curriculum, you must make a hundred-year plan by writing it on your heart, not just on paper. Let me explain. The little brain of your heart will make the big brain of your head remember anything that is truly important. I have recorded over 350 motivational hip-hop songs. I did not write a single one down on paper, because the words were just too important to me to ever forget.

In the business world, people spend months and, sometimes, years developing a business plan. They end up with pages and pages of ideas that hardly anybody wants to read and review. Your hundred-year plan is not something you can put in a filing cabinet, nor can you attach it to some email and forget about it.

What if you could take this hundred-year plan and turn it into a concise message and articulate it in under 30 seconds? The business world calls that an elevator pitch. Even investors don't want to read a long, boring business plan, but, if you have an elevator pitch, you can get someone's attention and, from that, build a relationship.

In his book, *Super Achievers*, founder of CEO Space International Berny Dhorman teaches, "Networking is the world's most valuable skillset."

Too many growing entrepreneurs and employees have mastered the art of talking themselves out of sales. That is why they use an elevator pitch to serve as a sales magnet during networking opportunities.

Imagine if you got on an elevator and were by yourself. Right as the doors were about to close, someone sticks their hand in between the doors, opening it back up. To your surprise, the person who steps on the elevator with you is someone you admire and respect. It is someone you felt like you were destined to partner with. An influencer who might be able to change your life and your family's lives forever. Clearly picture yourself alone on the elevator with that person. You know they are getting off the elevator soon. Now, here's my question: Would you have the courage to say something?

That is where the name originated from. In the studio days of Hollywood—before Netflix and YouTube— screenwriters would, supposedly, sometimes bump into people who could finance their films in an elevator. They had a captive audience member who could change their dynasty, and they didn't want to waste it. They had about 30 to 60—sometimes 118—seconds to share the idea of their movie and get people interested. To this day, if you want to get a film made in Hollywood, people won't read your script until they hear your short pitch.

While networking in business, an elevator pitch should consist of three pillars of information: *Who are you? What do you have? Why should I care?*

That's what's on the mind of a prospect when you first meet them. *Who are you? What do you have? Why should I care?*

The elevator pitch is the most effective networking tool, and networking is the world's most valuable skillset. As Mark McCormack reminds us in his classic book, *What They Don't Teach You at Harvard Business School*, "The best way to make a negative lasting impression, is to waste someone's time." The world of destiny is incredibly competitive. Most people listen with what's-in-it-for-me ears. I, too, am guilty of this. Unless you are pitching me on something, and I can see what is in it for me, I usually consider it a waste of time. I know it's wrong, but it's true of most high-achievers.

We have all been a victim of someone who has chatterbox disorder. People who seem like they have a marathon pitch, instead of an elevator pitch. We just pray that the doors of the elevator pitch open up and they stop talking. I'd like to call that a flying chair.

The first elevators are known to be used as early as 336 B.C. These early elevators were open cars, instead of closed ones, allowing groups of workers to move vertically higher than they could on their own.

Then, by the 17th century, King Louis XV was one of the first to use a dedicated passenger elevator. It was still very rudimentary. To make it work, there were men stationed in a chimney whose jobs were to pull on ropes. What a sucky job. At the time, it was hailed as innovative. When people saw the invention, they called it a 'flying chair'. Over-talking, while networking, and under-reaching is just as primitive. Next time you see somebody who talks you to death, tell them it's time for them to throw away their flying chair, and share that story of the King Louis the XV.

Your hundred-year plan should not turn into a flying chair, or some type of long, drawn-out process. After all, you must complete this assignment amid all the other responsibilities you have as a high-achiever. Believe me, the following exercise will not waste your time.

I have invented something I like to call a travelator pitch. Elisha Otis is known for inventing the elevators we currently use. I would like to be known for creating the travelator pitch. That can only happen if you execute the strategies that we cover in this chapter of the book. Before you graduate to your next level in life, I need you to develop your travelator pitch. Before I teach you how to make one, let's do a little more research into how modern elevators were made.

In 1823, two British architects innovated ropes and tugging, added a steam-powered engine to what was then called the 'ascending room', allowing them to take tourists to an elevated platform, so they could catch an epic view of London. Then, systems were developed that used water as a weight source to lift these cars up and down.

There were just two huge problems that stopped it from being popular: these elevator cars required deep pits and holes to be dug, and, the higher the elevator went up, the more impractical it was to have one. Also, they relied on cables that were known to snap and drop down to the bottom, killing any passengers and destroying any equipment on board. Then, Elisha Otis came along, making skyscrapers a possibility.

I bet he never imagined that his invention would transform into the official slang for the number one skillset. Mr. Otis started his humble beginnings as a straight-line thinking wagon driver. He got married and had two children, forcing him to become a blue-sky thinker. Once he and his family moved to another city, he invented a device that could turn corn and wheat into flour. Unfortunately, no one wanted to buy it. So, he converted that device into a sawmill to slice down log trees.

I'm sure he wanted to make a big impact for his family. It took a lot of hard work, but he could not attract customers. With two kids to feed, he went for the sure thing and began building wagons, like the one he started his career driving. He completely mastered what we will cover in your sophomore assignment. He didn't let the disappointments of his dream interfere with what his inner speech knew was his destiny. Suddenly, the call of conflict came crashing. His wife died, leaving Otis with two sons—one eight years old, and one still an infant.

I can't imagine the type of pressure he must have been under. Grieving for his wife while trying to figure out how to position a dynasty for his two sons. He didn't want them grow up to become wagon-drivers.

Eventually, he moved again, hoping for a fresh start. He ended up using his skills to make toys for a local doll company. He knew there had to be a better way.

Bored, he invented the robot turner, a machine that rapidly produced bedsteads. His boss gave him a $500 reward for his innovation. He was happy and hopeful. He used it as seed capital to start his own business.

The business never took off, but he took the medicine of defeat like a man. By this time, his two sons were young inventors, themselves, and helped him to design the first 'safety elevator.' It consisted of a brake that took charge whenever the cables snapped.

He offered it to the factory he was working at, free of charge, but they didn't give him a bonus for it. No orders came in for months. He must've thought that his destiny had peaked. But, then, his version of Harvard called. He was thrilled to see an advertisement about New York's World Fair, where he could showcase his innovation before a large crowd.

He decided to get on one of the platforms after installing his break, and, before an attentive audience, he ordered a man to cut the cable with an ax. The attendees were astonished when he did not plummet to his death. After that, orders took off, and that is how we got these things called elevators, making way for the term elevator pitch. Let us not get stuck in the past.

People who need elevator pitches are usually still in their destiny phase. When Elisha Otis had a volunteer slice that cable, he also sliced the cable of destiny and stepped right onto the travelator of dynasty.

A travelator is a moving walkway. You might have stood on one of these as you walked through the airport. I remember when I first saw one.

I was so happy to just stand on it and watch it move, rather than dragging my luggage the whole way. I think it is a lot more likely for a travelator pitch to connect with people than an elevator pitch. An elevator pitch is what you use to move up in your professional life. A travelator pitch is what we must use to move forward *beyond* our personal lives.

What's the difference? An effective elevator pitch always has three pillars for creation: *Who are you? What do you have? Why should we care?*

Imagine going through the airport and stepping on what you now know is a travelator. Right in front of you is someone you respect and admire. Someone you feel like you are destined to partner with. The only issue is, they're in front of you, and they are not standing still.

They have the combined speed of the machine and their natural pace, which is swifter than most. Would you have the courage to introduce yourself and present an opportunity to them that could impact future generations? Keep in mind, this is not an elevator-style interaction. Nothing is still. Everyone is moving. Once you master your travelator pitch, you will be prepared to seize the moment.

The first assignment is not to turn your hundred-year plan into a vision board or a grocery list. Rather, turn your hundred-year plan into a travelator pitch. This type of inner speech and outer speech can be stored in your mind and reviewed and updated on a regular basis. Your travelator pitch will propel you forward in ways that the elevator pitch simply cannot. Thank you, Mr. Otis, for inventing the car that takes people up. I want to be known one hundred years from now as the person who created the travelator pitch, and that the travelator pitch will be a tool that continues to move us forward in the present, so that we may be able to network with the future.

To turn your hundred-year plan into a travelator pitch, you must ask yourself three critical questions: *One hundred years from now, who have you reached? What impact will you have made? Why should someone I know get involved?*

Notice that your travelator pitch has very little to do with you. That is because when we are moving through life, people don't care how much you know, until they know how much you care. Who you are impacting and how it impacts them says a lot about you. Furthermore, your hundred-year plan is not limited by time, only imagination.

This allows for flexibility and compassion that the elevator pitch is missing. Sharing what you have is nice, but the impact made by what you have is much more valuable information. Finally, the ultimate call to action. *Why should someone I know get involved?*

You can't just make your travelator pitch for your inner speech. You must share it with others. After all, this is a tool to help us make a hundred-year plan, without massive overload. For you to execute your hundred-year plan, it will require you to get help from other qualified black-sky thinkers.

If you approach a stranger and ask them to help you complete your hundred-year plan, they might have you committed to a mental institution. Especially if they have Charcott-Wilbrandt syndrome and have forgotten how to dream. We can't expect people who don't even take their destiny seriously to take your dynasty seriously. That doesn't mean they can't help. It just means we must find a way to slice the cable of doubt from underneath them, and give them — or someone they know — something solid to stand on.

Let us compare an award-winning elevator pitch with a travelator pitch and notice the difference in impact. Then, I will give you the template, so that you can create your own. It should take no more than one hour to create a one-hundred-year plan. With a travelator pitch, one must simplify their ultimate dynasty by answering the three cardinal questions.

Katie Sunday won $1,500 first place prize in a business plan elevator pitch contest.

The winning pitch was this:

> "It would be nice if the males who develop iPhone apps for women understood us better. Ten million female iPhone users have repeatedly shown interest in the app market, but there are two problems here: 1) Not a lot of apps exist for women, and 2? Many of the apps that *do* exist kind of fall short of the mark. That's mainly because men are developing them. Our team believes we can connect with this dissatisfied and under-targeted market to bring very tailored apps, specifically for women. We are Ms. App, we are designing apps for women because women like technology, too."

Notice how she addressed the three pillars of an elevator pitch. But she did not answer the questions that a travelator pitch forces us to address. We don't know who she is impacting in the future, but, even worse, neither does she. Simply put, it doesn't speak to longevity. Your elevator pitch is all about the effect your business is having now. A travelator pitch is all about the effect your life will have on future generations. Chris Westfield is known as the elevator pitch champion and is the author of *The New Elevator Pitch*. According to Chris Westfield, "The old elevator pitch is a relic from a bygone era." Now, let us examine the template you will use to create your travelator pitch. The pitch of the future.

The elevator pitch is a tool to help take you up in business. A travelator pitch is a tool that can be used to move you forward towards your hundred-year plan. It will be the dynasty magnet that attracts black-sky thinkers to your team so that you can complete the three steps of making a hundred-year plan. Step one. Memorize your travelator pitch and here is the formula for you to create it.

Start off every time by saying,

One hundred years from now, I will be reaching _____.
Notice that the question is *not* who are you reaching now.

Who *will* you be affecting by then? Fill in the blanks as we go, and we can knock out your travelator pitch before we turn the page. You will be on your way to completing your freshman project.

One hundred years from now, I will have reached _____ (how many?) _____(who?). My _____ (what are you offering in the future?) will _____ (after) and _____ (before). Who do you know that wants to

_____,generationaftergeneration_____.

Here is a travelator pitch from business coach Akia Taylor. I asked Akia to think about her impact on the world one hundred years from now and answer the three magic questions that unlock the gates of dynasty. *Who have you reached? What impact will you make? Why should someone I know get involved.?*
We made her hundred-year plan in under twenty minutes. She said,

> One hundred years from now, I will have reached over 500,000 women. My coaching will help them to recognize their self-worth by overcoming the fear of their own voice. Who do you know that wants to provide incremental value for female leaders generation after generation and turn their spark into an inferno?"

We know what effect she is making on the future. We also can imagine who we might know in our network that may be a valuable collaboration for her. This is the same framework I have used for my travelator pitch. The same formula you will use to make yours.

My hundred-year plan says,

> One hundred years from now, I will have reached over 100,000 high-achievers. My motivational products will compel them to live bigger than the biggest ideas they have about themselves. Who do you know that wants to provide incremental value for high-achievers, generation after generation and turn their spark into an inferno?

To paraphrase my business coach, Ms. Akia Taylor, an elevator pitch is just a spark, but your travelator pitch is an inferno that can burn the cables of destiny and allow you to travel towards your dynasty.

Upgrade Your Mental Software

David Disalvo works as a writer for *Forbes* and has written a string of fascinating books about the brain. In one of my favorites, *Brain Changer: How Harnessing Your Brain's Power to Adapt Can Change your Life*, he says, "We've made more progress in understanding the brain and mind in the last thirty years than in all the time leading up to that point. Our mind is what our brains do, but they're also what other brains do; humans are mind-synced in ways we never realized."

The human mind is the most valuable software in the world. There is a term called neural coupling that occurs during what is now known as brainwave synchronization. When I hear this term, I began to picture an iPhone and a Mac computer. Everything on an iPhone is be synced with the user's Mac, and the two devices only fully work with each other. Brain-syncing allows for rapid learning, the same way that phone-syncing allows for rapid transfer of information between device and computer. We will enable neural coupling to take place between your travelator pitch and your second assignment as a freshman in the

H.A.R.V.A.R.D. Effect.

This next section of the book will help you gain more clarity. It will give you a visual guide to pair with your inner speech.

Planning is an important part of life. I have always had big goals in my mind, but, by joining an entrepreneurship club called CEO Space, I met people who actually wanted to help me with my ideas. It was astonished by how attentively people listened.

There was a couple named Trish and Steve, who were among the first to help me take my plan and put it in a mind-mapping system that I could understand. For your next assignment, you will learn how to use mind-mapping software to fill in the milestones on your hundred-year plan.

A one hundred-year plan is not a joke. It is a secret of some of the highest achievers who have ever walked this earth. After you memorize your travelator pitch, you are not done. There are at least two more steps to take before you can graduate to the next class.

One day at CEO Space, I had a meeting with a project manager, Trish. She was in her mid-forties, and she wore black glasses. I was telling her about many of the ideas for my business, and she asked me if I knew about xmind.net. Isn't it funny how there is always some new software out there that we are unaware of?

I downloaded the new software on my computer and found it very useful. Instead of looking at some words on a list, I got a chance to look at my core idea in the middle of the paper, as well as all the little bubbles stemming from that core idea. Trish turned my mind into a map. It had everything I had ever dreamed on it, and it was one page, so I didn't get too overwhelmed by it. I still have that original mind map today. There is only one problem. Everything I put on that mind map, every dream I had about my life, already came true.

I believe that mind-mapping is one of the most effective ways to plan for the future. Have you ever used mind-mapping technology before? If you have, then you are ahead of the game. This next assignment will be easier for you.

If you haven't used mind-mapping software, please don't panic and skip through to the next chapter. There is a sequence here, and, by now, you should have completed two projects that have been stored in your memory. 1) The memorization of the Harvard Creed. 2) The memorization of your travelator pitch. This next assignment will require you to choose a new software to learn, so that we can transform your ideas about your hundred-year plan into pictures.

When I sat down with Trish and we began to speak, I had no idea our minds were being synchronized. We will tackle the implications of mind-syncing when we cover the reverse-accountability section of this chapter.

One of the biggest ideas that was on my mind map was a television show. Within my first five years after making the mind map, I received two offers for a TV show. Both of them were not profitable enough to step away from my career as a speaker, so I declined. I'm glad I did. Soon, I found the perfect show. It allowed me to share my passion of making music. Together, with my cousin Kam Talbert, Joseph Gordon-Levitt, and an international crew of artists from around the world, we won an Emmy for the first season of *HitRecord on TV*. Now, two of us in the family had an Emmy. My dad won an Emmy for positive speaking. With the *HitRecord* team, I won an Emmy for positive rapping. When I heard the news, I instantly thought back to that mind map.

New studies about the brain shed light on why mind-mapping was so instrumental for me in achieving my goals. The book *Brain Rules*, by John Medina, teaches us, "We do not see with our eyes. We see with our brains." The challenging thing about creating a hundred-year plan is that we are carving out a future that is far beyond the reach of our eyes.

In *Brain Rules*, Medina discusses a research project done with a group of professional wine tasters. Researchers wanted to test the palate of these aficionados who make a living by their expert critique of fine wines. White wines and red wines require totally different descriptive words to explain their taste. They placed a tasteless die into the white wine, creating the appearance of the red wine.

None of the experts described the wine as white. According to the new brain rules of today, "Their visual inputs trump their other highly trained senses." The mind map you will be creating will serve as a dynasty die. This will trump your other highly skilled senses. When

Trish made that map for me, she tricked my mind into syncing up with my future, because I had a visual thinking tool. Your visual thinking tool will serve as your dynasty journal. All the ideas that pop in your head regarding your hundred-year plan will be visually represented in the software you will access.

Windows 95 was the computer software I grew up using, before I really knew what software was. I didn't know what to do with it. This was when the Internet required a landline connection. If someone was on the Internet, the phone line was busy. I saw what was happening outside the computer, but I had no concept of what the software was doing.

Before I tell you your options on the software you will use to create your century map, you'll be happy to know that you have many options to suit your learning style.

Whether you want to use your computer off the Internet to work on it while you are traveling, or online, where you can share it with black-sky visionaries from around the globe, the choice will be yours. Or, maybe you want to access the software from your trusty mobile device. I do all the above.

I can't imagine using Windows 95 software in the 21st century. If we still had to plug in a telephone cord to get on the Internet, it would be a total nightmare. There have been at least eleven versions of Windows since Windows 95. Programmed instructions stored in the memory of computers for execution by the processor. That is the definition of software.

Thanks to a woman known as "the enchantress of numbers," software became the edge of possibility. Every time you turn on your computer or phone, remember that you are interfacing with a Ada Lovelace's dynasty. In 1843, Ada Lovelace became the world's first computer programmer. Microsoft would not be formed until 132 years later.

Ms. Lovelace was a black-sky thinker from the 18th century. She died at the early age of 36. We don't have to buy a stamp and mail a letter every time we send someone a message, because she didn't allow the power of her life to die with her. I wanted to learn more about "the enchantress of numbers." Her mindset was much more advanced than the people of her time. She never got a chance to use Windows 95 or set up a website, but it would not have been possible for us to move into the digital age without her. Without what Ada Lovelace thought of in 1843, 13-year-old Bill Gates would never have been introduced to a computer in his classroom in 1968.

Now, I understand why, at the age of 60, Bill Gates has a hundred-year plan. Your best days don't have to be behind you. They can be in front of you. Actually, they can be so far in front of you that others have to execute them on your behalf. I was curious to know more about what made Ada Lovelace a black-sky thinker way back then.

Her story reminded me of Michael Mann. Before the engagement that made this book possible, I was introduced to the leaders in the graduate school's student government. Michael was the only team member in a wheelchair. For some reason, I didn't mind being insensitive, so I asked him, "Hey man, why aren't you walking?" In my mind, I guess it seemed like he might have been temporarily injured or something. After I said it, I realized that I had never asked anyone that question in the past. I didn't know why I asked him.

He told me he'd had surgery on his Achilles tendon. After I left the campus, Michael and I stayed in contact, and I became his speaker coach, giving me the opportunity to learn his full story. Michael Mann serves as the president of the Harvard Graduate and Professional Student Government, the only council that represents all twelve of the university's graduate schools. In one of our coaching sessions, he said, "When I was young, all of a sudden, people noticed that I started walking funny. Gradually, it got worse and worse, until, one morning, I woke up, and I couldn't move a muscle in my body. I could think, but I couldn't talk, and it became hard for me to breathe." As I heard this for the first time, I felt sad. I never heard of anything like that before. One day, you're living your life, and the next, you just can't move.

His mother rushed him to the hospital. He could hear what was going on, but he couldn't move. He was forced to listen as a team of doctors advised his mom to give him a tracheotomy, a surgical procedure durin which they slice a hole in your neck to insert a device, so someone can breathe without their mouth and nose.

All the doctors agreed. Except one. After the team of doctors left the room, one stayed behind and said, "I shouldn't be saying this—none of the other experts agree with me, but I think your son can overcome this on his own." Michael heard this, too. His mom had the black-sky wisdom to listen to that one doctor, and, a few months later, he began to write, then, talk, and, eventually walk again. He said, "I walked into school on the first day, and it felt awesome."

Just like Michael, Ada Lovelace was paralyzed for a short period during her childhood. She was on continuous bed rest for a year. Eventually, she could walk with crutches. With neither of her parents playing a prominent role in her life, she was raised by her grandmother. I think she became a black-sky thinker while she was on bedrest, because the first invention she worked on was to construct wings for herself. Yup—you heard me. 75 years before the Wright Brothers invented the airplane, Ada Lovelace made up her mind that flight was possible for her. She examined what materials she could use, including different types of metal and feathers. She studied birds to determine the right distance between wingspan, and she published her research and strategy in a book called *Flyology*. Her final step after the compass she knew she would need and the equipment used was to integrate steam into the art of flying.

If she were reading this book, she would learn how to put all those big ideas on a mind map. Her dynasty is still alive, but she isn't.

You must put your big ideas on your mind map in her honor. Can you do that? If not, close the book now. Drop out of the H.A.R.V.A.R.D. Effect, just like Mikal Mann dropped out of high school.

I'll share more about Mikal's phenomenal story in the next semester. There, I will share how Mikal went from being a high school dropout to becoming a candidate for a master's degree at Harvard Graduate School of Education and president of its student government. To this day, he doesn't have a high school diploma, nor a GED.

Before we can move forward, you have a dynasty assignment to complete. Let's shift our focus back to the mind-mapping software that will allow your hundred-year plan to be stored in a versatile, visual form.

There has not been an update in the software that we use to set goals since before the 18th century. When every motivational speaker takes the microphone, almost all of them have told us how important it is to have a plan, but very few have actually taught us a modern way of completing this effective task.

Humanity needs to invent a new pair of wings. Wings that will take our plans off bedrest. Wings that will serve as a crutch for us to soar through the future that we won't be able to visit. The time has come to upgrade of our mental software, by innovating our intentions.

Before any major software product is distributed to the public, it must complete the systems-development lifecycle. SDLC is the oldest framework for building information systems. This allows software engineers to systematize the intimidating task of software design. To move from destiny to dynasty, it will require you to make a hundred-year plan. That may seem intimidating. Therefore, you must complete the systems development life cycle to manage this vital first step, so that you can move forward, beyond the prints of your feet.

In life, there are footprints, fingerprints, and future prints. Your mind map will represent your unique imprint on the future. An ultra-long-term plan must be composed of a worthy information system. All the information in your mind about how you can make a global contribution can be put in a system. All the design work you will put in along the way will pay off big-time for generations to come.

Right now, I want you to choose your mind-mapping software. You can go to xmind.net and download it for free. Or, on your mobile device, you can go to your app store and type in *simple mind*. There is a free version and a paid version with extra features. Or, if you already have a Gmail account, you can add Mindmap through your Google apps, which will give you a version you can create on the Internet. The Mikal Mann inside you is going to love this.

We are still in the requirement-analysis phase of the systems development lifecycle of our hundred-year plan. Software project managers have learned the art of leading and monitoring software invention and evolution. That is what your major is for this semester. Once you follow my instructions and map out all your ideas that complement your travelator pitch, you will become a software project manager in your own right. The first job a software project manager is responsible for is figuring out the requirements to complete a successful roll-out.

This is usually when a successful project manager would ask you to think about what you want to get. That antiquated software programed the computer of our minds. We know that life is short, that it is important to get all you can out of life while you are here. But, in my black-sky opinion, the only way to get all you can out of life is to give all you can, even after death.

A hundred years from now, do you think the quality of life will improve? Will our schools still be using chalkboards or smartboards? Will our prisons be more overcrowded, or will we turn them into museums? Without your future print, how will the moms and dads of the world cope with the rapid change that is already on its way, thanks to us?

Our sons and daughters deserve more than tablets and toys to take into the tomorrows of tomorrow. They shouldn't have to scrub up the mess of their ancestors. Are you ready to reengineer the motor of your responsibility? Or will the global debt of today bankrupt the unborn?

You know that you have a dynasty when you can accept the fact that you are just as responsible for what happens to humanity, after you are gone, as you are responsible for yourself, while you are alive.

Reverse Accountability

In his speech about transforming the technology of human accomplishment, Gary Hamel said, "For the first time since the Industrial Revolution, you cannot build a company that is fit for the future, without building a company that is fit for human beings." Mr. Hamel argues that if we look at the best innovation in the past hundred years, the greatest innovation is management.

Just a century ago, manufacturing companies had fewer than ten employees. Then, the U.S. steel industry became the first billion-dollar market. When he mentioned

U.S. steel, it made me think of Napoleon Hill. Before he wrote the book that inspired Earl Nightingale, he had a meeting with the founder of the steel industry, Andrew Carnegie.

Andrew Carnegie started out as an immigrant, working in a cotton mill, where he made $1.20 per week. That would be a little over $30 a week today. In 1901, he built and sold American Steel Company for $450,000.000, all without a college education. That would be worth $370,000,000,000 today. Andrew Carnegie was the man responsible for the world's first success philosophy, *Sesame Street*, and steel industrialization.

Even though Mr. Carnegie gave away nearly 90 percent of his fortune to charity, he did not give Napoleon Hill even $1.20 a week, after hiring him to write what would, eventually, be called *Think and Grow Rich*. Young Napoleon grew up carrying a six-shooter pistol everywhere he went. Once his father remarried, Hill's stepmother, Martha, encouraged him to become as good with a typewriter as he was with his gun. He agreed, and, soon, he started working for a newspaper as a journalist. His first assignment was to interview Andrew Carnegie. Mr. Carnegie suggested that, without compensation, Napoleon should spend the next 20 years of his life developing a philosophy of achievement to empower the average man.

In the interview, Mr. Carnegie said, "It's a shame that each generation must find the way to success by trial and error, when the principles are really clear-cut." He opened his rolodex of high-achievers to Napoleon, but he didn't pay him. Mr. Hill was scraping to get by with his newspaper job, and, in his spare time, he would go to the homes of John D. Rockefeller, Henry Ford, Alexander Graham Bell, and some of the other highest achievers of that era.

Without funding from Carnegie, the billionaire philanthropist, Hill's friends and family criticized him a lot. Just as some friends may make fun of you, if they ever hear you whispering about some grandiose hundred-year plan. The fact remains that people like Tupac Shakur, Ada Lovelace, Earl Nightingale, Andrew Carnegie, and even Elisha Otis and Mamie Brown have managed to impact modern culture positively from beyond the grave. Let me share with you how Napoleon Hill's name got added to that list.

Even though he wasn't financially compensated for interviewing the tycoons of our time, he did have the opportunity to synchronize his thinking with a new quality of individuals. The thoughts in their heads while he interviewed them did not just go on paper, they also synchronized with his own thought, the same way an iPhone syncs with a Mac. If your head was computer hardware, the thoughts inside it would be the software. Remember, software is defined as programmed instructions stored in the memory for execution by the processor. Without the software, a computer is just an artifact. An empty shell. The same goes for the software in your head—your "thoughtware."

Software was made in the image of the human mind. The only difference between computer software and human thoughtware is that software constantly has a team of project managers upgrading the program. Many people allow their thoughtware to stagnate. Someone once said, "Few minds wear out, more rust out."

After surviving an assassination attempt and working with Presidents Woodrow Wilson and Theodore Roosevelt, Napoleon Hill did not have a dime. He knew the richest people in the world, but he had not yet known what it was like to be rich. Exposure to all that wisdom forced him to make a mental picture that was way bigger than his humble beginnings. A mental picture that was bigger than his own lifespan.

You must look at your life not as how you want it to end, but, instead, as the difference that you want your life to make in the world. Instead of picturing your life, from the time you are born to the time you die, visualize your dynasty as lasting from the time you were born to one hundred years from now. I call that reverse-actualization. Maslow taught us that self-actualization is to realize one's potential. Reverse-actualization is to realize one's potential, even after death. Eventually, Napoleon Hill published a book that has sold over 30 million copies worldwide and has created value in the lives of generation after generation of success warriors.

I was honored to speak at the Napoleon Hill foundation with my father. Afterwards, I spoke with best-selling author Greg Reid, who is the Napoleon Hill of our era. He said, "What everybody in the industry was talking about wasn't how great your speech was, it was how you took notes when your dad was speaking. We know you have heard him thousands of times, but you had the respect to take notes, anyway."

As you take notes about your hundred-year plan and place ideas on your mind map, keep in mind that execution will be sure to follow. So, before you start working on it by yourself, I suggest you think about one or more people who can hold you accountable for progress in your reverse-actualization. That means you must share your travelator pitch with them and get some ideas about what can go in your mind-mapping software.

Why is this important? Carnegie taught Napoleon Hill about brain synchronization, before scientists could prove it. He asked Andrew Carnegie in the interview, "What do you know about steel?"

Mr. Carnegie replied, "Nothing."

"Well, then,' Napoleon said, "How do you run the world's largest steel company?"

He said, "I have a mastermind alliance with people who have the specialized knowledge I don't possess." They were mind-synced.

Who will be your Carnegie? Who will be your Dr. who stays with you in the room of dynasty and gives you hope, even when others are clueless? Since the early 1900s, there has been a major update to the mastermind principle. Vineet Nayar and a team of 8,000 employees formed a mastermind alliance and invented this thing called reverse-accountability.

Your final freshman assignment after memorizing your travelator pitch and downloading your mind-mapping software is to find a reverse-accountability partner.

Vineet Nayar, the software project manager for this mastermind update said, "In 2005, our company was trapped in the rearview mirror. Obsolete, losing mindshare, marketshare, and talent share."

Do you know anyone who is trapped in the rearview mirror? Always looking back at what they have already done for themselves, instead of looking forward at what needs to be done to ensure the brightest future?

Vineet Nayar distributed all the secret strategies of the company to 8,000 of its employees, and provided an online forum, where anyone could make suggestions.

This was a large mastermind, and it produced a huge payoff. Reverse accountability was born, because Vineet took his eyes off the small rearview mirror and put his foot on the pedal of innovation.

Instead of top-down leadership—wherein supervisors only measure the employees, in his company, employees can anonymously rate their boss, as well as their boss's boss, online. This simple shift in culture helps them stay ahead of the curve and has turned them into one of the fastest growing most profitable companies in the world today.

Thank you, Mr. Nayar and your 8,000-member-strong mastermind alliance. I spoke of your example at Harvard. I told them, as I am telling you, the high-achieving reader, to find a reverse-accountability partner who will hold you to your hundred-year plan. Look backwards from your hundred-year plan to where you are today, not from where you were born.

In a language in which so many words are born with siblings that have identical meaning, the word accountability is an only child. It grew up with no other kids in the house to play with. I tried to find a synonym for it, but they all fall short. That is because accountability is an only child.

You know what they say about only children, don't you? Well, psychologists have found something called birth order and have studied its repercussions. Turns out, only children are higher achievers, because they don't have to deal with sibling rivalry or compete for the family resources. Accountability is the first-and-last-born child of eternity. Only children are also known to have more personality traits. I believe that accountability has at least three personality traits.

Personal Accountability is an introvert. Because she grew up playing by herself, she has no problem keeping to herself and b homebody. This allows us to make plans in secret, because w that we can achieve more by saying less about what we're doing to others.

Party Accountability is the life of the crowd. This party animal loves to gossip and be in the mix of accomplishment. Party accountability invented the dance move known as the mastermind principle. This allows us to report back to others and let them know all the details of our progress along the way.

Then, there's **reverse accountability, which** is the most mature personality trait in accountability. This is the trait where she is married and only thinking about the future. She doesn't party as much, but she does have an imagination that spices up her love life.

Who will be your partner that can pull you out of the rearview mirror? Who can you share your hundred-year plan with that can hold the vision with you? Your final assignment is to find a reverse-accountability partner. Every day you step forward in life, their job is to hold you accountable for your reverse-actualization.

A project manager named Trish became mine. Ada Lovelace had a reverse accountability partner by the name of Charles Babbage. Bill Gates had a partner named Paul Allen. Steve Jobs had Steve Wozniak. Sync your future with one or more black-sky people who can keep you focused forward on the edge of possibility. These three steps will transform you into a black-sky thinker, which will automatically update your thoughtware. That is how you complete your freshman project.

The rest of the book assumes that you have your foundation in place: a travelator pitch, a mind map, and a reverse-accountability partner. If you can't find a RAP, don't worry. In chapter 4, we will cover it in detail, in the section called relationship capital.

There is one essential ingredient to look for when choosing your RAP, which is what I will be calling your reverse-accountability partner from here on out. Make sure that they are as T.D. Jakes taught me as a child, "Similar in philosophy, but different in function."

He also said, "If you are the smartest person in your group, you need a new group." Make sure that your RAP partner is smarter than you.

Work on the mind map together, turning all the ideas into a map of future impact. This is the difference between a brainstorm and a perfect storm. A brainstorm is the idea dump of yesterday. That is the term used for creative problem-solving. It will require the perfect storm to impact generation after generation. A perfect storm can be used to describe events of unusual magnitude.

When 8,000 employees collaborate with the CEO and invent reverse-accountability, how can we call that a brainstorm? It is a result of a project with unusual magnitude. Imagine if, one hundred years from now, every company in America had a system that allowed employees to hold their bosses accountable. How much would that improve the quality of life for the children of our children?

Before we conclude this chapter and move forward with the execution strategy that will bring your hundred-year plan to life, remember that you won't be here to enjoy the fruits of your long-term impact. Let your imagination go wild. Don't limit it based on the modern possibilities.

Every assignment I have given thus far is something I have applied in my own life. I am happy to share parts of my hundred-year plan with you, to help you formulate yours. My RAP is my dad. I know I'm as lucky to have him as Napoleon Hill was to have Andrew Carnegie as an RAP.

One of the things we agreed on in our mind map was the idea of a thought leader little league. A century from now, mental athletes of all ages will have an association to showcase their intellectual muscles.

In the late 80s, I heard my dad say, "If we can have little league football teams, basketball teams, and baseball teams, we should be able to have little league oncologists, radiologists, and endocrinologists." I never forgot it. By the time 3017 comes around, the world will be ready for his idea. That is one of the plans of the future that we know will have incremental value for unborn high achievers.

You will be happy to know that one hundred years from now, just like they have elevator pitch competitions, there will be travelator exhibitions. At these exhibitions, the most effective planners of our time will showcase their century plan, and judges will reward those who have the most thoughtware imagination, instead of capital evaluation.

The music that I have kept in my private vault will be still earning royalties one hundred years from now, so that our kids grow up knowing more about Rockefeller and Carnegie than today's kids know about Jay-Z and Beyoncé. A century from now, my bones may be broken and my breath may be absent, but the truth that burns in my music will still be igniting the airwaves.

One hundred years from now, the H.A.R.V.A.R.D. Effect will have been translated into over 100 languages. From brail, to Mandarin, Portuguese, and Yoruba. I can imagine it being a required reading for high school kids one hundred years from now. A century from now, the First Family of Motivation will be on a holographic empowerment tour, delivering never-seen-before presentations from our never-ending arsenal of timeless insights.

I see a higher learning system that doesn't have a high-debt curriculum auditing my great-great-granddaughter's curiosity. A perfect storm is all we need to go from teaching our kids to learn the alphabet to teaching our kids to memorize the Harvard Creed. A perfect storm of hope for the diplomats for the future.

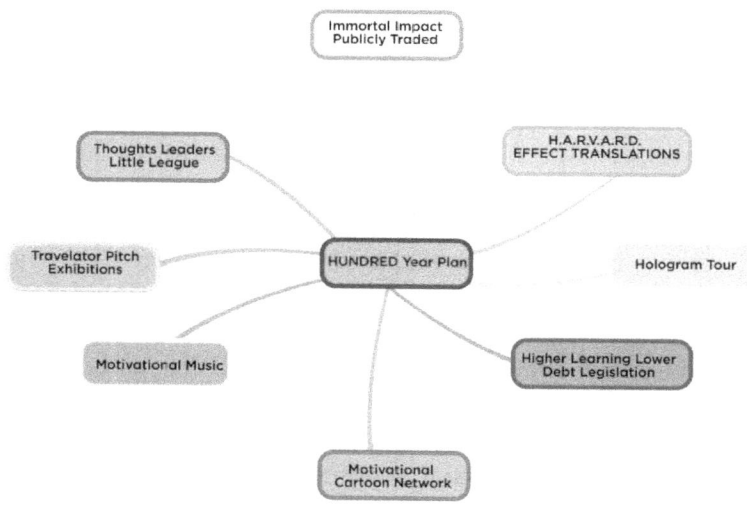

Notice how these ideas seem very far-fetched, but, somehow, on this mind map photo, it seems less intimidating. Without the limits of lifespace, all in achievement is possible. You and your RAP partner will make one with your great ideas.

After you have put down every idea—big, small, and even the seemingly silly—about what can impact generation after generation, you have officially done it. You have taken a monumental step forward by completing the requirement phase of the systems-development lifecycle. Review your mind map weekly, and constantly add updates and progress.

You can add text, pictures, and even audio and video to your mind map. Put all your effort into it, the same way Ada Lovelace mapped out her plan for flyology.

The world needs bigger, better, and faster planners. People whose ideas can benefit more than just themselves. I know that your hundred-year plan is going to be a creative, visual learning tool that will synchronize the how into your heart. Keep in mind, nothing on the plan has to include the knowledge or credentials to get it done.

Just as Andrew Carnegie did not know anything about steel. Your hundred-year plan might just be the one that turns cancer into a dinosaur. Your hundred-year plan might eliminate homelessness. Your hundred-year plan might involve resurrecting chivalry from the grave and teaching young men the long-lost art of being a gentleman.

No matter how huge you think when you are not limited to planning from birth to death, reverse-actualization does not require reason. It is a result of a perfect storm, wherein everything lines up just the right way.

The following chapters will be used to lay the foundation to bring everything you have in your black-sky mind to reality. While making plans, think big picture. Remember, when we look at the sky during the daytime, it is usually covered with clouds. Some people can't be creative in their planning, because they focus on the clouds, instead of the blue sky. But, then, if you've ever seen footage of space travel, you know that the sky that is beyond our solar system is not blue at all. It is a black sky, and most of us don't know it.

Your 100-year plan doesn't just change *what* you hope for, but *how* you hope for. When you change what and how you hope, you end up upgrading and changing who you are. This is the power you unleash in *this* moment.

The founder of CEO Space is Berny Dhorman. His father, Alan Dhorman, was a mentee of Napoleon Hill and Walt Disney. He grew up sitting on their laps. That is much of what turned me into a black-sky thinker and helped me realize my job is to learn, earn, and return. I remember hearing him tell the story about the day Disney World officially opened and how it was sad that Mr. Disney was not there to see it.

Someone clearly responded, "The only reason why we are all here is because he did see it before everyone else even thought it was possible." He couldn't see it with his eyes. He updated his thoughtware and saw it with his brain. I hope you have eternal dreams of fair dealings, because we are going to move to the next level and start working on our hundred-year plan. Today.

Allow Yourself to Fall

"Our greatest glory lies not in never failing, but in rising every time we fall"
-Vince Lombardi

It was my time. The moment that I had been anticipating. My speech was on point, like a ginsu blade. My navy-blue suit was crisp, like a new hundred-dollar bill. After Dean Lambert spoke about the history of success, it was my turn to talk about the future of success. They introduced me, and I ran to the stage like a track star. I was young, ready, and hungry to make a difference with my new message.

When I snatched the microphone from the podium, there was just one problem. My microphone would not work. The host tried to hand me a lavalier microphone, but, as a kid, I learned never to use one of those for a professional gig. They were asking me to break my family's cardinal rule, and I impolitely declined.

As a young lad, I fantasized about a lavalier mic. I am a very expressive communicator, so I wanted to speak with both hands free. My Dad told me that a handheld is always the way to go. I didn't believe him until we were at an event called "Engaged Today," where I had the pleasure of joining my him, Richard Branson, the founder of Virgin Airlines, and the Dalai Lama.

All the speakers on the program opted to use a lavalier. During an intermission, Les Brown was the only speaker who asked the soundman for a mic check. They offered him the little clip-on mic, and he impolitely declined. They quickly provided a handheld mic, and he walked on the stage and began to make sure that the acoustics in the room were just right.

I was in the back with the sound technicians. I heard one of them say to the other, "Oh, he's using a handheld? Handhelds always have a better sound quality. That is why he is the best." That day, my lavalier fantasy was over. I vowed never to use one again, if it could be prevented. I certainly wasn't going to use one at Harvard.

Now, I found myself before a silent crowd as my handheld microphone let me down. What else could I do? I couldn't use a lavalier and break my vow. I politely pulled the podium mic closer to my red tie and said, "It's okay. When they do give me the right microphone, I might just break it again." The audience respected my confidence during that stressful seven-minute slip-up, and they laughed out loud.

I remember feeling the uncertainty in the air. For a split second, I questioned myself again. Even though I had done so much preparation work, I could not anticipate the microphone not working during the most important speech of my life.

I walked away from the podium and began my classic introduction with only my moxie and guts to amplify my voice to reach the entire crowd. "It's your time," I said. I could immediately tell that the left side of the audience was more energetic than the right. "You know who I'm talking about. You!" I looked straight in the eyes of Mikal Mann in the front row, pointing at him, without using my fingers. I was trained to use my entire hand to single out an individual, instead of pointing a finger, I suppose as a way to be respectful.

"It's time to leave the stage behind and be real, and there's nothing real about what you're doing if you're lying to yourself. If you are lying to yourself and telling yourself that you can't make your hundred-year plan a reality, it's time to get real.

> This semester is going to be a real challenge for your ego. The main obstacle that stands in the way of you positioning your dynasty in life is the uncertainty about death. Someone once wrote, 'Death is the great final exam that we must all take.'"

Speaking of final exams, you will be asked to grade your own final exam in this chapter.

The book *Brain Changer* discusses what a powerful tool it is for the brain to write its own obituary. I will explain why later, but I just want you to be prepared for that uncomfortable assignment.

Many of us don't like doing things that make us uncomfortable, but, many times, comfort leads to conformity. That is why I fantasized about a lavalier microphone: it looked super-comfortable. Little did I know when I looked into Mikal's eyes on that day how comfort became the poison that took away the walking abilities that he had worked so hard to regain as a youth.

When Mikal started walking again and went back to school, he was a good student, but he fell in love with an older woman. That love inspired him to drop out of high school and work on the relationship full-time.

Eventually, he would go on to community college. He did well there, even without completing high school. He was good at doing his schoolwork; however, Mikal's doctor asked him to do leg exercises that would prevent the muscles in them from shrinking. He told me that he did not do them as often as he was supposed to, because they were difficult and t uncomfortable. He knew that if the exercises didn't work, he could just get a simple surgery and be in a wheelchair for six weeks, and, then, the problem would be solved for good.

The time came for the surgery, and everything appeared to be going as planned. After six weeks of sitting in the wheelchair, Michael said, "My dad picked me up from the chair and placed me directly on my two feet. When he did, I immediately fell straight to the ground."

The surgery that was meant to improve his walking ended up taking it away. Mikal failed to do those uncomfortable exercises and relied on the surgery to solve his problems, and that surgery let him down. Literally.

After speaking on the power of a hundred-year plan, I instructed the audience to repeat after me. "A." The audience echoed my passion. "'A' stands for, **A**llow yourself to fall."

Acting as my reverse-accountability partner, the day before the speech, my sister, Ona, suggested that I change *fail* to *fall*. Because of her, you won't have to sit through a bunch of pages talking about how failure is a necessary part of success. Forget about that lovey-dovey talk. Anyone who tells you to embrace failure is probably too successful to remember what failure truly tastes like.

To *fail* and to *fall* are very different. If success is the only choice for a Harvard

graduate student, they probably will learn very little about failure, but they will learn a lot about a thing called *fallure*. I'm not the only way who knows about fallure. Jim Collins, who wrote classics like *From Good to Great* and *Built to Last* also thought about fallure during a rock-climbing trip. To fall means to drop or come down freely under the influence of gravity.

Collins was attempting an on-site climb, which is described as a clean ascent, with no prior practice or beta. Jim came to a point on the rock where he did not know where the next boulder to place his hands was located. Because he had never traveled that path before, he was uncertain about the accurate path to the top. Like many of us when we are confronted with the uncertainty of unfamiliar terrain, he let go of the rock and allowed the rope and gravity to slide him back down to the bottom. He knew he had more energy and could have kept going, but he didn't. That is when he defined the difference between the inconspicuous *fallure* and his notorious, diabolical stepbrother *failure*.

Mr. Collins said he realized that failure is a conscious decision to give up; whereas, *fallure* is giving 100 percent, without knowing the outcome. To make a plan where you won't be alive to verify the outcome, it is important for us to overcome the fear of falling. It is one of the two fears we are born with as children. An infant's first two fears are loud sounds and falling. Let me break down this falling thing, so we can see why it's so important for us to do it.

One time, my best friend Wayne and I went to an Outkast concert with some friends. The Atlanta-based hip-hop duo had not been on tour in a while, and we were excited as we arrived at the jam-packed Staples Center in downtown Los Angeles. On the way to our seats, Wayne went to get something to drink, and, while walking towards the concession stand, he slipped and fell. My first reaction was the same as everyone else's reaction — I started to laugh.

Suddenly, I caught myself. I remembered being sick in seventh grade while spending the night at Wayne's house. He walked to 7-11 and got some chicken noodle soup and made it for me. That was my best friend on the ground. It was no longer funny. I instantly wiped the smirk off my face and ran towards him, to help him get back up. Just like Wayne, I did not see the nearly invisible vomit that forced my dress shoe to slide. Instead of coming to my best friends rescue, I ended up falling right beside him, landing in grossness. I spent the whole concert singing "I'm sorry, Ms. Jackson." I was thinking about how nasty it was for that throw-up to make me fall. Not once did I blame gravity.

When Mikal Mann fell after his six-week waiting period, I bet you he did not blame gravity. But, to fall means to come down freely under the influence of gravity. I was astonished to learn that gravity is the force that causes the tides of the ocean. Gravity allows the stars to shine bright. Gravity is the reason the earth orbits the sun and the moon to orbits the earth. The bigger the object is, the more gravity it exerts.

Even though we all exert gravity, the only thing that gravity does not majorly affect is subatomic particles.

If we plan to bring our black-sky visions to life, we can't do so without overcoming our ignorance of gravity. The first man to define gravity was Sir Isaac Newton. The greatest fall in scientific history came while Mr. Newton was doing some blue-sky thinking under an apple tree. He watched an apple fall, and the theory of gravity was born.

His theory was revolutionary, because, in 1687, it demystified the galaxy. Mr. Newton also invented the reflecting telescope and is the father of calculus. He has been heralded as one of the greatest scientific minds that ever existed. His theory—inspired by a simple apple—enabled astronauts to glide across the moon.

It is amazing how a small fall can turn into a groundbreaking discovery. Sometimes, we fail to recognize the hidden forces behind the physics of our lives. Gravity is a force in the universe. It means more than "What goes up must come down." For nearly 250 years, the world was content with Sir Isaac Newton's theory about gravity.

Everyone except patent clerk in Switzerland who was born over two centuries later. Albert was not known as a scientist, because no one would hire him. His job at the patent office was to review new inventions and simplify their meaning. There was even a time he thought his life was a failure. He wrote to his parents, "Perhaps, it would have been better if I were never born."

But Albert had an extraordinary imagination. One day, while riding a bus, he imagined himself moving at the speed of light. In his imaginative leap, he looked at the clock, and time was standing still. Then, he envisioned a man falling in an elevator, imaging that he would be weightless in the elevator if the cord snapped. This lead to a research paper that would eventually earn a Nobel Peace Prize.

Albert Einstein was 28 years old, working as a patent clerk, unable to get a job in the science community. It would take 15 years before the astronomers could verify the theory that came from his wild imagination that day. To check his equations, expedition teams would be sent to Australia, Africa, and California. Two times, the astronomers tried to capture photos, but there were too many clouds in the sky, blocking the view. Eventually, it was that same imagination that helped create the technology to launch satellites in space.

The imagination and the mathematics of these two men have helped generation after generation. Newton knew the force of gravity, Einstein understood the details about gravity. All this information has caused me to rethink falling.

Yes, gravity is a force of nature in the universe. The smaller a thing is, the less gravity it has. I believe we should analyze the apples that drop in our minds. I believe there is a such thing as mental gravity. Mental gravity is a force that we must be aware of while we ascend to our dynasty.

The bigger your ideas are, the more mental gravity you have working on your behalf. The worst thing that can happen after making your hundred-year plan is that you get too afraid of mental gravity to climb. Your dynasty is an on-site climb, meaning the terrain of this mountain will be unfamiliar to you. Remember, this task will require you to master the art of fallure.

Fallure is what connects the giants of all industries. The outcome may be unknown, but the impact of what the unknown can bring is often astonishing. I believe that when 28-year-old Albert realized that he had fallen into a lifestyle that was beneath his genius, it gave him the inspiration to be a groundbreaking individual.

The world needs more groundbreakers. People who are willing to change the answers to the questions we have asked the universe. If you see yourself as a groundbreaker, get ready for mental gravity. Mental gravity is a force that must be confronted. It means that the smaller the idea you have in your head, the less power it will have on earth. Don't be afraid of the size of your ideas. Size matters in this equation.

Small ideas don't even crack the sidewalk. The mass is not enough to make a dent in the ground. A big idea that serves others. A huge idea creates incremental value for future generations. That has mental gravity. That deserves to be seen on earth. We cannot be afraid of the mental gravity that governs the physics of our mind. We must execute 100 percent, without being aware of the outcome. There are three benefits of mental gravity, once we master the benefits of mental gravity we can overcome our fear and hesitation.

I first discovered mental gravity after I got the crazy idea to run for governor of California. Before my father ever became a bestselling author, or a globally known motivational speaker, he was a radio personality. After doing an editorial about a police officer who kicked a pregnant woman in the stomach and killed her unborn child, my dad was fired. This became a groundbreaking fall for our family.

My brother, Calvin, told me that, as a child, the phone at the house went from ringing 100 times a day to not ringing at all. Someone suggested that, since none of the other radio stations would hire him and he could not find a job, he should run for office as an Ohio state legislature. Without any previous experience, he went on to defeat a 22-year incumbent. I'm proud to say that he passed more legislation as a freshman elected official than anybody in the state of Ohio since.

Hearing him share those political stories from his past always inspired me as a child. I wasn't born when it happened, so I didn't get a chance to go door to door with my brothers, Calvin and Patrick. I just wish I could've been there for those historic family moments. I was inspired by starting my own family and becoming a father. I felt like political leadership was my purpose for being born.

I had never worked so hard in my life. I was at a dinner with a friend who suggested I run for governor. They were joking. I took it serious. I wanted to investigate what it took to run for a political office. I also wanted to know what the main duties for that office were. I was astonished to learn that the form to run for governor was shorter than the signup process for an email address.

I did the research. I made a plan. I raised money. I did everything I could do. I got help from everyone I possibly knew. I remember getting a call from the *L.A. Times* for an endorsement meeting. I walked into that building with full-color printed copies of my campaign strategy over three election cycles. I was utterly underimpressed by the simple questions that were asked of me after so much study and research was put into my preparation. I was ready to carry the torch in politics. I was ready to lose, if necessary. What happened ended up being the biggest fall of my life.

Even though I paid to be on the ballot and filled out the right forms in Sacramento,

I had to get a certain number of signatures to fully make it on the ballot. The deadline came, and I turned in the signatures, which my team and I knew were more than enough. After celebrating and making plans to launch a campaign, the clerk's office called and left a message. Some of our signatures should have been turned into Orange County, not Los Angeles County.

I came three signatures short of making it on the ballot. Just three signatures, and there was nothing I could do about it. It felt like all the work and money I had put in had been wasted, trying to reach for something beyond my comfort zone. Without that fall, I would not be able to write this book. That fall taught me about how to handle the first effect of mental gravity.

When mental gravity pulls you down under its influence, it will make you react. How you react and how you handle the great devastations that mental gravity provides when it takes control will determine whether you will become a ground-breaker. Some people want to break the ground; most people want to just stay above the ground. Only one is possible for mankind.

A ground-breaker is someone who has learned how to channel the power of mental gravity. They use the mass of big ideas to make an even bigger impact with their lives. A groundbreaking thinker is not afraid of fallure. They don't have to focus on all the things that could go wrong. They are averse to risk, because the outcome is unknowable at times.

While confronted with the heaviness of rejection, they lift their shoulders higher. When they are tackled by doubt and criticism, somehow, they plow through the tunnel of pessimism to the other side of glory. Groundbreakers are the gladiators of innovation. I hope your hundred-year plan is groundbreaking. How do we manage the disappointment that comes when mental gravity kicks in?

First and foremost, mental gravity can make people angry. Anger is a powerful emotion. I was sad when I didn't make it on the ballot, but I was also angry. Angry at myself for even trying. In my mind, I had climbed to the top of the political food, but mental gravity bought me tumbling right back down.

That anger made me realize that I didn't have to be in higher office to make a higher difference. I do, however, have to apply that same commitment that I had while running to a worthy enterprise that does more than tell people to think positive. Execute on site! You will thrive as long as you execute. Allow yourself to find a new reason to get angry.

I need you to get angry when mental gravity tells you that your hundred-year plan is a waste of time. It's okay to channel your anger into a formula that shatters people's belief systems about what they think you can achieve. The highest human achievement is the ability to reduce inequity. We need some groundbreaking leaders to get angry and use their anger as fuel for innovation.

When is the last time that you got angry? Do you think you have the emotional maturity to transmute anger into something positive? Anger can consume you, or it can propel you. If you can't lose your temper in a constructive way, fallure can bully you into never climbing again. Using uncertainty as an excuse not to reach for the boulder that you've never seen before.

Tony Teegarden wrote, "By surrendering on the shores of knowing myself, I don't struggle to break free from the gravity of my mind, but only to set sail on the wave of possibilities that wash upon it." Your project for this semester might make you angry at me. It will cause you to surrender on the shores of knowing yourself. I want you to fall on the waves of possibility. Fear not mental gravity, for it will give you the critical mass to be a full-time groundbreaker. Surrender to the anger inside you. Anger can trigger the fight-or-flight response that can propel you to great achievement.

Too many high-achievers allow their comfort to outperform their anger. We need people who are willing to fight to make the world a better place. Not just for their own benefit. We need people who aren't so in love with succeeding that they become afraid of falling.

During a time of war, Albert Einstein was betrayed. All his colleagues decided to support Germany's war. Albert was asked to sign his name as a supporter, which him furious. He was not afraid to speak out against the war. His anger saved him from being on the wrong side of history. He decided to create a counter-petition of professors who were in support of peace. Less than ten people signed. He was alone. But his anger triggered the power of his ethics.

Ethical anger is, perhaps, the greatest energy-booster not sold in local convenience stores. To harness the power of anger, we cannot sweep it under our intellectual rugs. We must surrender to our ethical anger in a way that unleashes a perfect storm.

Anger is known as the emotion that hurts others. I think we should repurpose that power. If anger is strong enough to do something to harm others, I think it can also be strong enough to help others. Anger has done enough harm in the history books. Let us use anger's might and power to clean up his own mess. Zora Neal Hurston said, "Grab the broom of anger, and drive off the beast of fear." Sometimes, anger forces us to be bolder than we thought we were. Your anger can put fear in a beast that once put fear in you.

Aristotle and Dr. Wayne Dyer have wonderful views about anger. Wayne Dyer said, "There is nothing wrong with anger, provided you use it constructively." I plan to use my anger constructively. I'm angry that Wayne Dyer is no longer here with us. My father and he were supposed to meet to discuss doing a PBS special together. I had his number in my phone, but I never used it. I surrender to the ethical anger inside me and that pushes me to make a PBS special, in honor of Wayne Dyer.

One day, when you are flipping through your television stations and you see my red tie and red glasses on a PBS special, know that I surrendered to my anger and stopped acting like it didn't exist. Aristotle once wrote "Anybody can become angry - that is easy, but to be angry with the right person and to the right degree and at the right time and for the right purpose, and in the right way - that is not within everybody's power and is not easy."

It will not be easy to surrender to your anger. It takes a high EQ to know when is the right time to fight or take flight. I don't want you to get angry at little things that happen to you. I want you to get filled with anger about the big ideas that you have inside you, and figure out a way to do something about it.

Will you run away from a challenge that benefits more than you? Will you cower to the doubt of uncertainty? Or can you use your ethical anger to fight the battle of time and leave a mark on the world that won't be wiped away by your absence?

Sydney J. Harris said, "If a small thing has the power to make you angry, does that not indicate something about your size?" What is one big thing you can use as a reason to get angry? To trigger the fight-or-flight response that will make you bolder than you've ever been. This groundbreaking emotion has done enough harm. Let us now use its strength to do good.

Science shows us that there are at least 21 different types of anger. Unfortunately, only one type of anger can make a positive impact. If you use the wrong type of anger, it can take you backwards. Let's cover the 20 types of anger that are toxic. Behavioral, passive, verbal, self-inflicted, volatile, chronic, judgmental, overwhelmed, retaliatory, paranoid, deliberate, avoidant, sneaky, sudden, shame-based, addictive, habitual, moral, hate, and violent anger. If you find yourself with any one of these types of anger, just pump the brakes. These forms of anger have done enough damage to society.

I remember when I became the survivor of a hate crime. My friend, Arias, and I went to a house party with his girlfriend. It was, perhaps, the most boring party in history, so we left early. While crossing the street on the way to the car, a car approached us and almost hit us. We jumped out of the street and looked back as to see why the car did not slow down while we were crossing. The five young men in the car were angry, because of our ethnicity.

One of them rolled down the window and yelled, "What are you niggers doing around here?' I had never witnessed this type of anger before. Two chased us on foot, while the car pursued. I separated from Arias and his girlfriend, hoping they could get away. I thought that maybe the five angry Hispanic young men would follow me instead. I remember asking myself what they would do to Arias's girlfriend if they caught her. My quick plan worked. Now, they were only chasing me. I ran for my life. I wish I could say that I was brave and stood my ground. The truth is, I thought If they caught up with me, it might be fatal. So, I ran for my life.

I was running so fast my Gucci Timberlands flew off my feet, leaving me running barefoot. There was no one around to ask for help. I thought I cut a corner where they could not see me, but I was wrong. I fell in a bush. The car pulled up and the men of pulled out baseball bats. I thought it was my last day on earth.

The bat came down as I was coming out of the bush, hitting me directly in my left eye, permanently blinding me. After Arias got his then girlfriend safely into the car, he came back for me. Arias came back, screaming angrily and acting as though he had a weapon. His anger from watching me get beat up became the force that scared away the assailants.

After I was safe, they took me back upstairs to the boring house party. Arias gave me his t-shirt to catch the blood that was dripping from my face. We got upstairs, and I removed the shirt. Everyone in the party said, "Damn" at the same time, like a scene out of a scripted sitcom.

They rushed me to the hospital, where I got 20 stitches in my head. While getting my stitches, a police officer came in to take my statement.

This is when I got to choose my anger. The one type of anger that we need in the world to undo the abuse that we have endured as a global village. I chose constructive anger. Constructive anger is the feeling of being fed up with how things are going, and the need to make a positive change. I did not want to press charges. I wanted to press forward and make a positive charge in society.

If I had died that day, or even allowed a different type of anger to change who I was, I would've missed out on giving the best speech of my life at Harvard University. And, perhaps, the H.A.R.V.A.R.D. Effect would only be accessible to its students. Thank you, constructive anger, for challenging me to make a bigger difference, and for granting me the wisdom not to let the disease of hate infect my spirit.

If I could speak to my attackers, I would ask them to read this book, because anger is an unavoidable ally. We must use our anger as a motivating force to make a positive change.

I still don't have sight in my left eye, but my vision is even bigger than before. Was I angry at those gentlemen for calling us names and threatening our lives? Yes. Do I get angry when I get medical bills or go to see my eye specialist and they tell me there's nothing else they can do for me? Yes. My constructive anger pushes me forward. Anything else would be a waste of greatness.

Henk Aarts and his research team at Utrecht University in the Netherlands found that anger stimulates the left parts of the brain that are associated with positive emotions. They also conducted a research study that proved how anger can motivate you to go after something. Each participant was asked to watch a computer screens that presented different objects. What they didn't know was that, subliminally, pictures of either fear, neutral, or angry flashes were flashed before each object, attaching an emotion to each one. The participants were asked to squeeze a hand, indicating how much they wanted the object.

The unconscious influence of anger caused most of the participants to pick the objects that came right after anger. The participants did not respond the same way with objects that presented fear or neutral subliminal messages. Henk Aarts said of the study, "It shows how little we know, about our own motivations," because the participants were not even aware that their wants were influenced by the unavoidable emotion of anger.

Here are two examples of how two men in the same family can use anger in ways that are constructive and destructive. Thomas Lincoln was just an eight-year-old boy. One day while on the farm with his brothers and father, a Native American took his dad's life, right in front of him, leaving him in shock. His brother ran into the house to get a weapon. Right as Thomas was about to be snatched up by his father's assassin, his eldest brother, Mordercai, saved his life.

Now that the father was gone, all the wealth and land was passed to the eldest son. The year was 1786. Mordercai inherited a fortune, but Thomas was left with nothing. He did not have an education and, at eight years old, he had to start working and earning his own way on different farms.

Eventually, Thomas saved up enough to buy his own farm and start a family. He had a daughter and son. His son loved books, but Thomas was illiterate, so, he preferred to see his son working on the farm than reading or learning. This must've angered Thomas that his life was so hard and his brothers was so easy. He took that anger out on his intelligent son. He would whip him for reading or hide—and, sometimes, destroy—his books. His son, Abraham, would be contracted to work long hard days for other farmers, and Thomas would keep all the earnings for himself.

His son, Abraham, felt like a slave as a child as a result of the way his dad worked him without pay and abused him physically. Abraham was determined to constructively use the anger he had towards his father. Although he had less than one year of formal education, he went on to become a lawyer. When he ran for office and lost the first time, he allowed himself to fall, butitdid not stop him from creating a political legacy that all our children study in their schools. Thomas Lincoln could never have imagined that his anger and mistreatment towards his son would be used as momentum to turn Abraham Lincoln into one of the most beloved figures in American history.
Thomas Lincoln's anger was used to abuse. Abraham Lincoln's constructive anger was used to emancipate. Two members of the same family who each have a totally different legacy. All because they used anger in different ways. I knew that it was a long-shot for me to be elected into office. I knew that, even once I got my name on the ballot, I would be an unknown with no political background or major backing. I know that politics is a dirty game, in which people like to discredit you and look for a scandal.

I thought back in history at how important political leadership is to have in society, and I got angry that there were not more options. I got angry of watching political news in disgust. Constantly being asked to choose between the lesser of two evils. Looking at our so-called leaders bicker like brats on a playground, rarely standing shoulder-to-shoulder on common ground. My constructive anger at mental gravity gave me the momentum needed to press forward in ways that created multiple personal and professional groundbreaking rewards.

Remember that fallure is not failure. I thought that my life was over after my name did not make it on the ballot. I can relate to the patent clerk, Einstein, and, even though I did not say it, I wondered if it would have been better if I were never born. I did not have the same respect that I do today for mental gravity. I thought I failed on that day. I thought I let my entire family down. My best friend, Wayne, was there for me every step of the way. He got more signatures than anyone. When I told him the terrible news, all he said was, "I'm proud of you, for doing your best." He told me that I was an inspiration to him, not because of what I had failed to do, but because I did not allow a fear of falling to overpower my desire to climb.

Courage Is an Ancient Currency

The second thing that mental gravity can affect is your attitude. This next assignment is guaranteed to impact your attitude about your dynasty. Attitude is a result of your self-narrative. Attitude is the anchor of your self-expression. If there was a way to get through the H.A.R.V.A.R.D. Effect without mentioning that age-old word, trust me,

I would.

But, when it comes to falling, we need to turn mental gravity into momentum. Is it possible to turn a terrible fall into a groundbreaking achievement? All the greatest achievers do it. How do they do it? That is, of course, the question.

The first slipped step of falling asks us to surrender to our anger. Once you do that, it is important to be in constant defense of your attitude. Attitude is the great senior citizen among us. For generations, it has developed a stellar reputation when it comes to success.

The theme of the event that day at Harvard was that success is the only choice. That is not just a statement; it's an attitude. After my departure from the campus that day, my look and dress remaind the same, but, ever since I set foot on that beautiful campus, I have developed a different attitude. Not just about myself, but, also, about the type of contribution that I think can be made in this world. All the falling I had done in my life did not stop me from learning about the H.A.R.V.A.R.D. effect. In fact, it propelled me.

This next assignment will prepare you for the worst thing that could ever happen to you. It will also force you to use mental gravity as a weight to sum up your entire life. I am going to take you through the step-by-step process of how to write an obituary for your dynasty. What do I mean by that?

When a person's spirit leaves their body, there is usually a funeral service to honor their memory. These services are attended by the loved ones of the deceased. Just like my grandmother's funeral, someone else will usually write and read an obituary in their honor. This 500-word essay forces one to take full responsibility, to tell the last chapter of one's life story. The obituary is supposed to sum up a person's life meaning.

I want you to develop a new attitude about your hundred-year plan. Nothing is more of a downer than thinking about one's death. Therefore, I don't want you to write your obituary for where your life is now. That can only center around your past. I want you to use this mental gravity experiment to write an obituary for your dynasty 100 years from now.

After the impact, what will people remember most about your dynasty? Who will show up, to remember the good and bad times that were generated by your ideas? Usually, we pass on this grim task to our close friends and loved ones. Your obituary is, perhaps, the most important 500-word assignment of our lives. Why delegate that responsibility to others?

In his book *Have the Last Say: Capturing your Legacy in One Small Story*, Alan Gelg lists five reasons why we should craft this critical essay ourselves. I can relate, because, initially, I hired a ghostwriter to complete this book. When the person I paid to didn't deliver, I got angry. Then, I had to defend my attitude about this project, so that it did not remain incomplete.

I was not going to let anyone rob me of the story I needed to tell. That is when it hit me. No one can ghostwrite your dynasty on your behalf. It is too important to leave in the hands of an independent contractor. Your obituary has the same type of value. Take charge of your life story, and unleash all the benefits that mental gravity provides.

Here are at least five of the benefits of "Having the Last Say," according to Alan Gelg:

Resolve, perspective, accuracy, acceptance, and connection. These gifts will dramatically shift your attitude about your hundred-year plan and the sum of your life. Innovate on your intention for the meaning of your life, because it is impossible to remain uninfluenced by this mental gravity experiment.

Here are a few biographies of high-achievers that are sure to inspire you to make your life count in a bigger more dynamic manner. Let us first look at the obituary of the late, great Maya Angelou.

THE OBITUARY OF DR. MAYA ANGELOU

Dr. Maya Angelou was born to Vivian Baxter and Bailey Johnson in St. Louis, Missouri on April 4, 1928. She passed to her Heavenly Reward quietly on May 28, 2014, in her home in Winston-Salem, North Carolina. She is survived by her son, daughter-in-law, two grandsons and two great-grandchildren, a nephew, a niece, grandnieces, great-grandnieces, grandnephews, great-grandnephews and a host of beloveds.

From the time she was a child, Dr. Angelou proved that she was a unique individual with amazing commitment and focus. The birth of her son, when she was seventeen, did not prevent her from continuing in pursuit of her dreams for a creative career. From her start as a singer in San Francisco's Purple Onion and Hungry I in 1953 to the installation of her portrait in the Smithsonian National Portrait Gallery in Washington, D.C. in 2014, she was continuously on a dramatic, musical or political stage.

She was a dancer, a singer, an actress, a poet, a writer, a magazine editor, a playwright, a film director as well as a college lecturer, full professor, and a fearless, outspoken activist. She never let her various vocations inhibit her activism or her willingness to speak out against injustice and inequality. She performed in a number of major productions. She was in both the 1954 International Touring Company and the subsequent movie of *Porgy and Bess*. She was also in the 1977 television series of Alex Haley's *Roots* and in the 1995 film *How to Make an American Quilt*. She was in too many other productions to name. She directed the films Georgia, Georgia and
Down in the Delta.

Her first book, *I Know Why the Caged Bird Sings*, was published in 1970. She went on to write thirty-five other books including autobiographies, poetry, and essays. A number of her works were best sellers and were published in a number of languages.

Throughout her life, Dr. Angelou's activism never flagged or wanted. In 1959, during the height of the Civil Rights Movement, she headed the New York office of Dr. Martin Luther King's Southern Christian Leadership Conference. Next, she worked for the *Arab Observer News Magazine* in Cairo, Egypt, which was the of English language magazine in the Middle East. Later she moved to Ghana and met Malcolm X. She returned to the United States to work for him, but he was assassinated four days after her arrival in New York. She continued to be a voice of humanity, speaking out against anything that fettered the human spirit. Her life and her body of literary work trumpet the importance of love, tolerance and forgiveness. She was a warrior for truth, justice, and love.

Notice how it does not mention her being raped as a little girl. She told my dad the story how, as a child, she told her family her mother's boyfriend was abusing her. Her family's violent anger killed him. This violent anger had a dramatic effect on her attitude. As a little girl, Maya Angelou became known as a mute. It wasn't until many years later when her grandmother, Annie Henderson, encouraged her to use her gift of speech again.

She had seen how her voice could have a deadly impact. Her grandmother forced her to shift her attitude and use a gift that would go on to inspire multiple generations. If she had never spoken a word again, imagine how different her life would have been. Her Mamie Brown, Annie Henderson, would have said to her, "Sister, Momma don't care what these people say, that you must be an idiot, a moron because you can't talk. Momma don't care. Momma know that when you and the good Lord get ready, you gon' be a teacher."

In an article by *Smithsonian Magazine*, she recounts the great attitude lessons her grandmother gave her whenever what she called "complainers" would come into the store their family owned. She said as soon as a complainer would come in and spread the gossip about all the bad news that was happening in their lives, she would turn to young Maya and say these powerful words, "There are people all over the world who went to sleep last night who did not wake again. Their beds have become their cooling boards; their blankets have become their winding sheets. They would give anything for just five minutes of what she was complaining about."

This influence developed in Maya Angelou a form of courage that few humans master. Her fearless attitude was not just used for her personal gain. She was a voice for the voiceless. There is no other like her in history, and there will be no other version of you. Take charge of your self-narrative, just like Maya Angelou began to take charge of her voice, a voice that was used to empower the hopeless.

Your dynasty obituary will focus not on what you have already accomplished. Instead, it will focus on what will be achieved by you a hundred years from where you are today. You have the luxury of choosing the date and place of your death, not for your physical death, but for the death of your dynasty. I want you to see it end, so that you can begin to measure your attitude and defend your new self-narrative. Just as it did for Ms. Angelou, it is going to require an attitude of courage. In her 1993 Presidential Inaugural Address, "On the Pulse of The Morning," she wrote, "History, despite its wrenching pain, cannot be unlived, but if faced with courage, need not be lived again."

One day, when I was sitting in the audience at one of my dad's seminars, he told the audience that "Knowledge is the new currency." That is true. The dynasty obituary that you will write will give you a new currency about yourself. There are some products in life that we cannot purchase with all the might of the dollar bill. Euros and yen cannot pay off mental gravity from knocking on your imagination's door. We need you to connect more with the self you want to know in the future. It is then that you are connected with the self-narrative you have developed, based on your past.

Mona Simpson, the sister of inventor and futurist Steve Jobs, said," Death didn't happen to Steve, he achieved it!" The inventor of the iPod might not have written his obituary, but he did make sure that each participant at his memorial service received a brown box. In each box was a book, called *Autobiography of A Yogi*. Mark Benioff, the CEO of Salesforce was there. He said, "That was his message, actualize yourself....

He had this incredible realization that his intuition was his greatest gift, and he needed to look at the world from inside out."

For your reverse-actualization, it takes a massive attitude adjustment to give the task ahead the necessary energy to break through the tests of time. You must learn how to defend your attitude with the great ancient currency. Yes, knowledge is the new currency. The playing field has been leveled, and those with knowledge get first dibs on creating their ideal lifestyles. But, before knowledge was the new currency, history demonstrates how courage served as an ancient currency.

When knowledge wants to skip out on the bill, courage is always there to pick up the tab. Way before Wall Street existed or bitcoins were around, courage was the angel investor that bought our society forward.

Defend your attitude with courage. It takes courage to turn the giant of criticism into a cockroach. To adopt a courageous attitude towards life, and to summarize your life's meaning for yourself. To have the last say in your story.

Here is your assignment: Courage is the great defender of attitude. Will you complete this mental gravity experiment and reap the benefits that only few who have walked the earth have dared to narrate?

It took me almost a week to complete this assignment. It forced me to adjust my attitude about death, which has made me reexamine the purpose of my life.

Aaron Joseph Purmont wanted the final say in his story. It was a humorous one. They did end up reading this at his funeral. He was not famous, nor was he some international icon, but he was a world-class father. Here is the obituary he wrote for himself:

> Purmort, Aaron Joseph age 35, died peacefully at home on November 25 after complications from a radioactive spider bite that led to years of crime-fighting and a years-long battle with a nefarious criminal named Cancer, who has plagued our society for far too long. Civilians will recognize him best as Spider-Man, and thank him for his many years of service protecting our city. His family knew him only as a kind and mild-

mannered Art Director, a designer of websites and t-shirts, and concert posters who always had the right cardigan and the right thing to say (even if it was wildly inappropriate). Aaron was known for his long, entertaining stories, which he loved to repeat often. In high school, he was in the band The Asparagus Children, which reached critical acclaim in the northern suburbs. As an adult, he graduated from the College of Visual Arts (which also died an untimely death recently) and worked in several agencies around Minneapolis, settling in as an Interactive Associate

Creative Director at Colle + McVoy. Aaron was a comic book aficionado, a pop-culture encyclopedia and always the most fun person at any party. He is survived by his parents Bill and Kim Kuhlmeyer, father Mark Purmort (Patricia, Autumn, Aly), sisters Erika and Nicole, first wife Gwen Stefani, current wife Nora and their son

Ralph, who will grow up to avenge his father's untimely death.

Instead of writing about your past, write about your future. Use your wildest imagination, and use this mental gravity experiment to say the best goodbye you can.

Here is a copy of my dynasty obituary. I hope it inspires you to make an even better one. Self-actualization asks you to look at the time you were born to the time you die. Remember that reverse actualization asks you to look at your life one hundred years from now, to the time that you were born.

John-Leslie Brown's dynasty passed on July 4, 2117, in a private compound in Kauai, Hawaii. He was born to Lajaune Bryant and Les Brown in Detroit, Michigan on May 22, 1984. His dynasty is survived by his son, Honor Phoenix Brown, eleven brothers and sisters, ten nieces and nephews, and loved ones.

From the time he was a child, John-Leslie demonstrated that he was not afraid to use his voice. By the year 2067, his dynasty helped developed a new global industry of modern inspirational products, resulting in an international positive peer pressure campaign that has created an uprising of millennial-owned-and-operated campuses. These information achievement centers have reimagined the best strategies for rapid learning and implementing in a borderless economy. Although he ran for higher office 21 times and lost, The Personal Motivation Act of 2097 served as a major victory for him, helping to create the type of economic boom unparalleled since the late 1990s.

His goal of updating the software of planning inspired him to work with a talented team of engineers to architect revolutionary mind-mapping software that millions of people use daily, helping servant leaders to make better short-term decisions that impact their long-term life plan. When his only son graduated from Harvard University, he became the happiest dad on the planet.

The H.A.R.V.A.R.D. Effect, his first book, which was dedicated to his son, became one of the top 100 most influential books of the century, according to *Rolling Stone*. He would go on to write ten others, including *If the Future's Broke, Just Fix It*, and *Hunger Will Never Die*, which were also turned into short films that captured the attention and the imagination of high-achievers from all walks of life.

Quietly, he was always looking for a way to better his best, going out of his way to do something positive for others. But, when he was asked to host the 157th Grammy Awards, the whole world knew that both his music and his speeches were something that pop culture was craving. He is the first motivational speaker to be inducted into the Rock and Roll Hall of Fame for his smash hit "Immortal Love Letters."

John-Leslie Brown's dynasty was that of a life-changing speaker, a ground-breaking hip-hop artist, a distinguished author, an underrated actor, a contemporary filmmaker, a coach to the coaches, and an agitator to the complacent. He never let his knowledge of the possible get in the way of his curiosity about the impossible, leading him to spend his early years as a philanthropist splitting half of his estate between his son and his non-profit ventures. One of these ventures has capitalized on a new market of thought leaders, who compete globally in an online league that rewards the ideas that can make a long-term positive value. He started something special, but he wants you to remember that it's not over, until you win.

Start out with choosing your ideal resting place for your dynasty. What day of the year did your dynasty pass away? Where was your dynasty's home base? After that, comes your parents and your date of birth.

So many people have an immortal attitude towards life. We think that death does not apply to us. I'm saying make a hundred-year plan. If you didn't have eternity or a thousand years to make you dynasty come alive, if your ripple into the future is limited to 36,500 days. If your entire dynasty statement is limited to 876,000 hours, summarized by 500 words.

Japan has the world's highest life expectancy of 80 years old. America is currently 34th on this list. You may not be able to predict your actual death, and I don't know why you would want to; however, you can determine when your dynasty is born and let the people who survive you determine when it dies. If you surpass the century mark, great. But, for now, say goodbye in the future and imagine that you lived up to your hundred-year plan.

> Full name, including nickname, Age at death
> Residence (for example, the name of the city) at death day and date of death (remember to include the year) at place of death
>
> Cause of
> death LIFE
>
> Date of birth
> Place of birth
> Names of parents
>
> Childhood: siblings, stories, schools, friends
> Marriage(s): date, place, name of spouse
> Education: school, college, university, other
> Designations, awards, and other recognition

Employment: jobs, activities, stories, colleagues, satisfactions, promotions, hobbies, sports, interests, activities, and other enjoyment

Charitable, religious, fraternal, political, and other affiliations; positions held

Achievements
Disappointments

Unusual attributes, humor, other stories
FAMILY

Survived by:
Spouse

Children (in order of date of birth, and their spouses)

Grandchildren

Great-grandchildren

Great-great-grandchildren

Siblings (in order of date of birth)

Others, such as nephews, nieces, cousins, in-laws

Friends

It's impossible to complete this assignment without having it affect your attitude. After your new attitude about your hundred-year plan is established, it will affect not only your attitude towards yourself and your future, but, also, your attitude towards others.

Mastery Loves Company

One of the biggest mistakes high-achievers make every day is defending their narrative by attacking someone else's. Many of us think that, if we are successful enough, we have earned a license to treat those who are not however we see fit.

Sometimes, we must humble ourselves for the sake of someone else's feelings. There is a quote that says, "When it comes to choosing between being right or being kind, always be kind." Defend your attitude about your future. Don't let anyone interfere with your new self-narrative. Keep in mind that having a robust attitude requires you to have the strength to know how to admit when you've made an error.

Dennis Waitley is the author of the "Psychology of Winning," one of the best-selling audio series of all time. He met the late Earl Nightingale, and Mr. Nightingale released Mr. Waitley's first audio series in 1978. He still remembers Tony Robbins as an 18-year-old kid. He is like the Eminem of the success industry.

I first met Mr. Waitley while speaking before 8,000 people at a conference in Salt Lake City. I had only four minutes to do my entire presentation. When I finished this short presentation, I noticed that only one person in the audience gave me a standing ovation. It was Dennis Waitley. A master in our industry. He had no idea what his kindness has meant to me.

I had the pleasure of sharing the stage with him as he was getting inducted into the Self-Help Hall of Fame at the Habitudes Conference in San Diego, California just one day before my speech at Harvard. I was so surprised to hear him talk about how most people don't recognize him, even though he has sold millions of books and helped tens of thousands of people. He says whenever he is in a public place, people mistake him as a waiter or employee, because of how he dresses. Dark suit, red tie. He said people are often trying to hand him keys to a car, as if he were a valet driver, or asking him to take their order in a restaurant. I was shocked. This guy is a living legend to me. I don't think I could be as kind as he is if I were being confused as the help. But, when I shared his wisdom from that during the allow yourself to fall section of my speech in Boston, it struck a chord. Remember, Dennis Waitley said, "Humility is not humiliation."

All the masters of marketplace have experienced a dance with humility. Travis Kalineck was the keynote speaker in 2011 at a conference called Failcon. Failcon is a conference for founders of organizations that helps them prepare for failure, so they can grow faster. Travis' presentation talked about how he considers himself to be the unluckiest entrepreneur in the world.

Travis started his journey of entrepreneurship while at college at UCLA. He did extraordinarily well on the SATs, and, after coaching a student and helping them improve their score 500 points, someone suggested he make it a business. He soon became bored, even though he was teaching most of the neighborhood. He wanted a bigger dynasty.

Determined to use his background in computer science, he built a company that he knew would be huge. It was a search engine that would bring up any download of any major entertainer. He finally found a major investor, but it was an exclusive deal, and the investor ended up suing Travis for trying to raise more money elsewhere. The negative press disrupted a multi-million-dollar opportunity with AOL.

He was also sued for twenty-five trillion dollars by all the major media companies. Travis was forced to file for bankruptcy. His dream was crushed. He learned that his cofounder and most of his software managers resigned and began working at Google. Travis said he is not a pioneer of technology, rather, he is a pioneer of failure. Those falls would force him to come up with something totally different.

Travis Kalanick was told that the there was nothing else to innovate in the software world. Those humble experiences served him well. He thought about how cool it would be to push a button and get a ride anywhere in the world. Travis Kalinick turned that trillion-dollar fall into a billion-dollar innovation. He is currently the founder and CEO of the ridesharing app called Uber.

Falling can either make you miserable, or it can transform you into a master. I can recall the day that I got my first investor. To have someone invest in my career as an artist and speaker was a big deal for me. Just like Travis, I thought the road ahead would be easy from that point on. I had never heard of *due diligence* before.

I ended up partnering with a multimillionaire who had no integrity. There would be no return for that investor, because the partner I chose had no intention of upholding the contract we formed. I was devastated. I have to admit that mental gravity got the best of me. With tears falling down my face, I would lie in the bed at night and ask the universe, *Why me? How could someone do this to me?* In retrospect, I can discern that it happened not so that I could become companions with misery, but, rather, so that I could master the art of fallure.

I almost allowed that challenge to break my hope for the future. Now, I wear that mental gravity experiment as a tattoo of strength. In 1905, President Theodore Roosevelt said during his inaugural address, "There is no good reason why we should fear the future, but there is every reason why we should face it seriously, neither hiding from ourselves the gravity of the problems before us nor fearing to approach those problems with the unbending, unflinching purpose to solve them aright."

Now I know what it means to be unflinching. Uber would not exist if it was not for anger and attitude. Surrender to your anger. Defend your Attitude. Overthrow with action. That is the final lesson that fallure guides us through, How to overthrow an entire industry with anger, attitude and action. The trifecta of fallure.

The groundbreaking dynasty that you were born to initiate requires unbending action. Where a trillion-dollar lawsuit or toxic business relationship does not prohibit your contribution. Stay in the arena.

During his second inaugural speech, Mr. Roosevelt said,

> It is not the critic who counts; not the man who points out how the strong man stumbles, or where the doer of deeds could have done them better. The credit belongs to the man who is actually in the arena, whose face is marred by dust and sweat and blood; who strives valiantly; who errs, who comes short again and again, because there is no effort without error and shortcoming; but who does actually strive to do the deeds; who knows great enthusiasms, the great devotions; who spends himself in a worthy cause; who at the best knows in the end the triumph of high achievement, and who at the worst, if he fails, at least fails while daring greatly, so that his place shall never be with those cold and timid souls who neither know victory

nor defeat.

Even though I have fallen many times, I have learned what it takes to stay in the arena. I will fight to spin myself in a worthy cause. I won't run away from a challenge. What is the master mindset? Fall while daring greatly. That is true mastery.

What the world needs now is not more students, teachers, or speakers. We need more masters. Masters go to sleep at night, unable to articulate their ideas to straight-line thinkers. Masters are criticized by their family members because they are not limited by their genepool. What is something that you will be known as a master for 100 years from now that you have no clue how to do today? There lies your new community. We are awaiting your invitation.

I remember speaking as a teenager in front of a star-studded audience. When I returned to my seat, I saw that Magic Johnson was sitting right behind me. He kept tapping me on my shoulder and encouraging me. Even though the program wasn't over, he kept poking me to explain how tremendous of an opportunity I had for being such a young voice of hope. After the event, Denzel Washington, Stevie Wonder, and Magic Johnson pulled me into a private room and gave me a test.

Mr. Denzel Washington—one of my favorite actors became one of the first mentors who really impacted my mindset—put nine dots on a sheet of paper in the shape of a square and asked me to connect all the dots without lifting my pen. I had no clue why this was important to him. I also didn't know how to pass the test that he was giving me before these masters of industry. After I struggled for a bit, he showed me that the only way to complete the exercise was by drawing outside of the box.

He wanted me to graduate to mastery. They all were trying to get me to see the unseeable. To see beyond what was in front of me. I might have been young, but I hold those brief moments dear to my heart. When you allow yourself to fall, you will, eventually, learn that mastery loves company. It can be lonely at the apex of dynasty. The brightest in the world would love to see your spark. Don't abandon their expectations. Surpass them. Go outside the lines of what your life has colored before. Take the actions that no one else is even thinking yet.

What if Travis would have never taken action on Uber, because he allowed the stress of failure to get the best of him? Even Einstein would have died as a patent clerk, were it not for anger attitude and action. He overthrew the world of science.

Upset a new market place, and be exposed to a family of doers that need your help to propel them even further. By the time I became a father, I knew it was time for a change. When my son, Honor, was born, I knew it was going to take new actions to be the best parent I could be. This was the scariest responsibility I have ever encountered. Having another human being to mold and love.

I love my son more and more every time I look into his eyes. When he was born, I was the first face he saw the very first time his beautiful eyes opened. I still remember how soft his nails were when he first squeezed my finger. They were so soft, they curled up on me.

I used to question if I could handle that major responsibility. Not just to be a role model, but to be an enrollment model that he could, one day, be proud of. As proud as I am of Lajaune Bryant and Les Brown. Well, now that young Honor is almost three years old, the fear of being an unmarried single father is the least of my worries. For my son, success is the only choice. I know that he will have to fight his own battles. But, as soon as he is old enough to understand, I will remind him that the credit belongs to the man who is actually in the arena.

RESOURCE MANAGEMENT

"Management is efficiency in climbing the ladder of success; leadership determines whether the ladder is leaning against the right wall."
-Steven Covey

What distinguishes a leader from a follower? A trendsetter from a consumer? Is it the way they were raised, or the teachers they might have learned from? Leadership is a result of management. The ones who are considered the most trustworthy to accept the responsibility of leading others in the corporate world have been labeled management. Great managers get more responsibility, less work, and better pay. Why is that?

When you can learn how to lead yourself, you also will learn how to manage the productive movements of others. Leadership is the gateway drug for profitable management addiction. As a sophomore in the H.A.R.V.A.R.D. Effect , you will learn the latest leadership management techniques that will ensure that you don't become a slave to your ambition, but, instead, become a general in the battles of epic desire.

As you continue to fall forward towards your hundred-year plan, begin to see yourself as a leader. You are mastering the H.A.R.V.A.R.D. Effect. This process will demand exemplary management skills. Many times, when mental gravity strikes and people are ready to surrender to their anger and defend their attitudes. When it's time to overthrow with action it can be tough to discern the best course.

There I was on stage, and the sweat was starting to pour. I had hustled so hard to maximize this opportunity. So far, it was going great. I talked to them about the hundred-year plan, they got the picture.

Then, I talked about the power of fallure. I was not sure how it would be received, because I had never shared my political story with an audience before that day. I could tell that it was effective.

In the book *Average Is Over,* Tyler Cowen writes "In today's global economy here is what is scarce. 1. Quality land and natural resources. 2. Intellectual property, or good ideas about what should be produced and 3. Quality labor with unique skills."

Average individuals do not have a hundred-year plan, therefore, they have every right to depend on the leadership of others. Tyler Cowen insists that average is over. The one thing that is scarce in a global economy is the one thing that made Harvard University interested in hearing what I had to say. Intellectual Property.

Peter Drucker said, "Knowledge has to be improved, challenged and increased constantly or it vanishes." For my mind to architect a new message for that audience, it forced me to improve, challenge and increase the knowledge I had of transformational principals.

Intellectual property pays all my bills. My intellectual property puts pampers on my son's behind and Nutri-Grain bars in his belly. I am fortunate to have a foothold in a multibillion-dollar industry that forces me to construct relevant empowering platforms of intellectual property.

While allowing myself to fall as a recording artist, there was not a day that went by where my dad's words didn't echo in my mind, "John-Leslie, you are not an entertainer, you are an intellectual resource."

When you want to buy physical property, it is often determined by the natural resources. Natural resources are everything you see in this world that is not manmade. The economic growth of a nation often depends on abundance of natural resources. Just imagine what the world would look like if all we ever saw was just natural resources, and there were no manmade inventions.

It is almost unimaginable to think back that far. For most of us, physical labor is a thing of the past. Everything that you see that is manmade is a result of supernatural resources. Water is a natural resource. Your mind can be a supernatural servant.

Supernatural means departing from what is usual or normal, especially to appear to transcend the laws of nature. It is nearly impossible to explain all the wonders that have originated from the mind, just as it is nearly impossible to describe the gift of air. There are three supernatural resources that we must manage properly to have the durability that is not limited to lifespan.

In the entertainment industry, there is a term known as one-hit wonder. It is used to label an act that has one big hit and is promptly forgotten. Even though they had the necessary skillset to make it to the top, their mindset doesn't keep them there. This is a worst-case life scenario.

There are also one-hit wonders in life. People who confuse temporary progress as permanent success. I want you to begin to look at your leadership skills in three areas. Keep in mind that as a resource manager, it will require lifelong adjustments to your leadership skills to make sure that your strategies endure.

Own Your Mental Equity

Those who go on to make more than one hit in life must not allow outsiders to occupy their intellectual property. This is what is scarce in the global economy, because many of us have allowed others to be the landlords of our thoughts.

When you stop thinking for yourself, and rely on the status quo to be your compass, you neglect the supernatural resource of your own mind. Your mind is the most powerful supernatural resource on the planet. How do you properly manage 70,000 thoughts a day? According to the Laboratory of Neuro Imaging at the University of Southern California, the average person thinks 48.6 thoughts per minute.

If you are not the owner of your property and are just renting it, you must pay someone else for their rights. The same happens with our minds. Some people forfeit their own mental power, by renting over 25,000,000 thoughts a year to someone or something else. What a waste. I think it starts when we're children. Hand-me-down ideas that we inherit and take with us into adulthood.

When I first got the news that I would become a father, all my thoughts began to focus on the negative aspects of fatherhood. I was more worried about how much parenthood would cost me, instead of how it could enrich me. When I was a kid, I often heard stories of drama between co-parents. I leased someone else's ideas, before I had any clue about the truth.

Veritas is the ancient Greek word for truth. It is also the motto of Harvard University. Owning your mental equity means that you manage the resource of every thought that pops in your head.

Many people feel that money is the most important resource to acquire in life. Money is also the mother of most one-hit wonders. If you are rich in money and poor in ideas, the wealth will evaporate quicker than it was formed. The fact is, your thoughts are worth more than any coin or paper bill.

There are many types of thinking, just as there are many forms of money. The type of thinking that is best suited for leadership is estimation thinking. If you want to buy something on a plane, you can't pay cash, no matter how much you have on you. They only accept credit card. Leadership is the product that cannot be purchased with logic. It requires estimation thinking.

I want you to begin to take charge of those 48 thoughts per minute. Repurpose your thinking style. When a person estimates, it requires them to pull from whatever data is available to produce possible data that does not currently exist.

All your thoughts have electrical power, but not all thoughts were created equal. I feel like the ones among us who are known for reaching new territories are those whohave mastered the electric power of estimation.
Sometimes, we can be on autopilot in life, where all the thinking we engage in is narrowly focused on activities with a precise result. Our life stops being an adventure, and we stop using our estimation skills. Logic requires explanation skills, but leadership demands estimation skills.

If you can spend more of your 25 million thoughts per year estimating, you can afford to learn the H.A.R.V.A.R.D. Effect. Don't waste your time trying to find an explanation for everything. The fact of the matter is, dynasty is unexplainable. Focus your mind on thoughts that give you information to make better estimations. For our sake, there are two types of estimations that make a big difference between owning your mental equity and leasing somebody else's.

My sister, Ona Brown, is an estimation expert. When I was a little kid, she would have imaginary dinners with world-class leaders, and tell me all about it. I thought she was a little weird. She was establishing a new truth for herself. She wanted to trigger the thoughts in her mind that she would have if her heroes and sheroes attended her private dinner parties.

With very little data, she estimated that, one day, she would meet these heroes, so she decided to get some early practice. One of those heroes she often invited to her imaginary dinners was Nelson Mandela. Ona is a vegetarian, so she would prepare an elaborate boca salad. She would burn some candles and have soothing music playing. She would focus her thinking. Instead of watching television, she would entertain the masters of our time.

When my sister would talk to these imaginary guests, she couldn't explain why. Now, I know she was estimating. What should she wear for such an honor? What type of mood would need to be set in herself to share a special moment with greatness?

Well, it paid off. She heard about a delegation going to South Africa to hear Nelson Mandela speak. She called my dad and asked if he would pay for her to join the delegation, but he refused. He believes that if you give a woman a fish, she'll eat for a day, but, if you teach her *how* to fish, she'll eat for a lifetime. Ona estimated that if she left 30 messages on my dad's voicemail explaining how important this opportunity was, he would give her some fish. Her estimation was wrong this time.

Even though she was unable to explain how she would get to South Africa, she estimated that if she could make it to the motherland, she would be able to meet one of her heroes. She ended up reserving her ticket with the delegation, without having the money to pay for it. At the last minute, the delegation covered her expenses, because they had extra money in the budget.

After arriving on the continent, using only the resource of her mind, she was standing outside of an event where Mr. Mandela was to speak. This is a man who had been imprisoned for 27 years and who estimated that his imprisonment could, one day, lead to his presidency. He estimated that his country needed a leader who was not willing to compromise with oppression. There Ona was, closer than she had ever been to one of her imaginary dinner guests. The only problem was the place was sold-out, and there appeared to be no way for her to get an up-close and personal introduction.

That is when she heard someone say, "Ona, Ona Brown, is that you?" She turned around to see who it was. It was Reverend Michael Beckwith, a family friend. Reverend Beckwith was supposed to be sitting in the front row. He asked if Ona could help him get through the crowd and get to the front. He said he would find a seat for her as well.

Ona instantly turned into Moses and began to urgently part her way through the crowd. After they arrived to the front, Mr. Beckwith was called to the back, to meet Nelson Mandela, and asked if Ona wanted to join him. Right before he went on stage, Nelson Mandela went over to Ona, said, "Hello," and gave her a kiss on the cheek. All those imaginary dinner parties paid off, *big-time*.

To own your mental equity, you must overestimate your *veritas*.

Your truth. The mind is your supernatural truth-maker. Don't take it lightly. If you can overestimate your own truth, your mind will not be led by self-esteem, it will be led by your self-estimation.

Before a homeowner purchases property, they send someone out to estimate the property value. Each one of your 48 thoughts per minute have a value attached to it. If you don't estimate which thoughts have more value, your mental equity will become worthless.

Once you identify the most valuable ideas that you can produce, you must consciously act to own those properties. Estimate the value of each thought you have, and observe where each thought could lead.

Eve Branson knew this power far too well. She was determined to be a fighter pilot in a time when women were not allowed to vote yet alone serve in the military. She went down to where all the soldiers were stationed. She noticed that the pilots all wore leather jackets. She began to overestimate her own truth, thinking that if she got a leather jacket and cut her hair, maybe she could blend in. For weeks, she practiced talking in a deep voice, because, even though that job position was only for men, she estimated that, if she didn't tell them she was a woman, the other soldiers wouldn't notice.

Eve's overestimation led her straight to the cockpit. She never knew that her young son would inherit her same overestimation skills and go on to one day own his own airlines. Eve Branson's son is Richard Branson, the owner of Virgin airlines. Look how her intellectual property inspired her son to value his own thoughts differently. His mental equity has generated him a personal net worth of over five billion dollars.

The most valuable thoughts are those that make us increase our self-estimation. A leader knows how to overestimate themselves. When you intentionally overestimate your truth, it forces you to overthrow previous truths about yourself.

Ernest Hemingway wrote, "There is nothing noble in being superior to your fellow man; true nobility is being superior to your former self." Noble estimation is the key to superior leadership.

Let us focus most of our thought power on the ideas that give us better data for a new estimation of ourselves. When you've come to a point at which you feel no more calculating needs to be done, you are in big trouble. The days of retirement are a myth. There used to be a time when average people could work the same job their whole lives and retire on a percentage of their income. Our parents have been forced to re-estimate their value in their later years. It takes a special kind of thought leader who knows how to maintain their mental equity.

In the pursuit of happiness, beware of the thoughts that occupy your intellectual property. Some thoughts have turned into tenants that need to be evicted. Some ideas have yet to pay off and are several months behind on providing recognizable value.

The Latin word *colere*, meaning 'to inhabit,' is where the word colonization comes from. When a country is colonized, a central entity comes in and takes possession of all the natural resources. Global colonization is the root of war and destruction in many societies. However, mental colonization is the most vicious crime known to mankind.

Most of the terrible violence that we see on a global scale has negatively impacted the indigenous people, who did not have the resources to defend themselves from the powers that be. Your ideas are an indigenous community. They have certain rights that they have earned, due to their historical ties to a particular territory. Entertainment, pessimism, guilt; all these imperial forces can turn into mental colonizers, if you don't properly manage your super natural resources.

None of us can control the earth. We might not have dominion over the weather or political climate. We do, however, have complete control of our minds. There are 196 countries in the world. Over 90 percent of these countries have been colonized by an outside force. We can learn about how to avoid mental colonization by studying one of the few nations that has never been subjected to foreign rule.

Bhutan is a nation that is known as the happiest country in Asia. It has never been Colonized, due to the leadership and resource management of the Wangchuck dynasty. The Wangchuck Dynasty began 110 years ago. Since 1907, the House of Wangchuck has passed power forward generation after generation.

Let me share with you one of the grandest political conspiracies in the history of leadership. A *Lama*, which is a term that means master teacher, by the name of Ngaywang Namgal was the founder of the Bhutan state in the 15th century. He is known for establishing a dual system of government, also known as a diacracy. This empowered local governors, as well as religious officials.

The Lama is one entity who was supposed to be replaced by another incarnation. When Mr. Mamgal died in 1651, the leaders of the dual system kept his death a secret for over 50 years. They thought if the public knew of his death, it would turn society into chaos, so they said he was on a spiritual retreat and issued orders in his name.

When the secret was revealed, the remaining members of the diacracy divided the duties into three separate incarnations, instead of just one common leader. These incarnations were known as the mind, the body, and the speech.

According to Wikipedia, the country would have internal wars for the next 200 years, until the Wangchuck Dynasty was formed. The body incarnation did not last very long. It died out in the 18th century. The mind and speech incarnations lasted into the 20th century. Ultimately, the power from the speech incarnation became the king.

At the age of 16, after the death of his father, Jigme Singye Wangchuck became the leader of Bhutan. He would go on to introduce a concept to the United Nations that sets the standard for managing the supernatural resource of our minds. Usually, when countries measure the success of their nation, they are narrowly focused on something called the GDP — the gross domestic product — of their land.

In 1972, the young leader from Bhutan argued that Gross Domestic Product is not a measure of human well-being, it is simply a measure of goods and services exchanged in a marketplace at a given time in a given country. It is based on the idea that in measuring "wealth," only economic development is considered.

Thus, the concept of GNH was born. Gross National Happiness. In July 2011, the General Assembly of the United Nations passed Resolution 65/309, unanimously adopting GNH.

Since William Petty first developed the concept of GDP, no one has dared challenge how we estimate the success of our societies. It took a member of the Wangchuck Dynasty, over 300 years later, to invent a modern estimation approach. Just think about it: what is the point of having a lot of products produced and sold in a society as the only estimate of progress? What does that do to the supernatural resource of human beings? We are more than the services that we buy and sell. We were put here to be happy, not just to be hard workers.

When we manage the resource of the intellectual properties in our minds, let us borrow the GNH approach. Estimate the Gross National Happiness that each idea provides. Making a product is a talent.

Happiness is a skill. Happiness is a powerful alternative indicator. In the science of happiness, we learn how important our mental resource is. Created by UC Berkeley's Greater Good Science Center, one of the fundamental finding from positive psychology: that happiness is inextricably linked to having strong social ties and contributing to something bigger than yourself — the greater good.

Previous generations were told that happiness is a choice, but cutting-edge research into the science of happiness reveals that happiness is not a choice, but a skill. Let's dig a little deeper, so that we can truly understand the concept of GNH.

In the field of psychology, there were over 54,000 articles about depression between the years of 1967 and the year 2000. There were only 1,700 articles about happiness.

It turns out, when you look at the whole field of psychology, there is a 21:1 ratio in favor of negative psychology There were over 41,000 articles about anxiety, but only 415 research papers about joy.

Dr. Martin Seligman, who was the president of the American Psychological Association, became the father of the positive psychology. When interviewed by CNN, Dr. Seligman was told that he would have three words to answer the following question. "Dr. Seligman, what is the state of psychology today?" He said, "Not good enough."

He believed that the business of making miserable people less miserable is not good enough. Eliminating depression is not the same as elevating to happiness.

The science of psychology was focused on disease. Not necessarily development. It studied more about schizophrenia than it did genius. Dr. Seligman is known for saying, "Psychology should be just as concerned with strength as it is with weakness. It should be as concerned with building the best things in life as it is with repairing the worst. It should be as concerned with making the lives of normal people more fulfilling, and with nurturing high talent, as it is with healing pathology."

I think the evidence that he discovered fully supports the value of what the Wangchuck Dynasty has presented the United Nations. In the Declaration of Independence, it reminds us that, "We hold these truths to be sacred & undeniable; that all men are created equal & independent, that from that equal creation they derive rights inherent and inalienable, among which are the preservation of life, & liberty, & the pursuit of happiness."

Use your mind to pursue gross national happiness. Happiness is 50 percent genetic, 10 percent environment, and 40 percent intention. Your mindset represents 40 percent of your happiness. Make sure you don't waste the resource of your mind. Pursue ideas that make you happy, because a world with high Gross Domestic Product sales and low Gross National Happiness is a world that is not good enough.

Despite growing up in happy households, there was a point in my teenage years when I found myself unhappy. At times, touring alone at an early age can be a lonely journey. Gross Happiness was very low, even though I was raised on the highest of self-help curriculums. It wasn't until I was punished by my dad that I started to do the eternal work that allowed me to use my supernatural resources to the fullest.

Motivators are not born, they are groomed. Even though I was groomed since birth to motivate others, there were times when I allowed my mind to be influenced by depression. I have been one of the most fortunate kids in the world to have my parents' genetic predisposition for happiness. But that is only half of the battle. I have even been exposed to a rare quality environment, but we know now that genetics and environment combined only account for 60 percent of a person's gross happiness.

Your assignment this semester is a lot more difficult than it sounds. It requires us to answer a typical question in an unorthodox fashion. One question that all human beings get asked on a regular basis is, *How are you?*

When you get asked this question, what is your response? Most people say, *Good*. Sometimes, we answer this question on autopilot, and we never seize the opportunity to spread gross national happiness.

As a young man, whenever I heard my dad being asked the question. "How are you?" He never replied in a traditional manner. A major part of owning your mental equity and not permitting your intellectual properties to be colonized by outside forces is taking charge of how you answer this question. Just think about it. How many times would you estimate that you have been asked how you are?

My dad would always answer the question like this, "I am better than good and better than most and, sometimes, even better than that." Your trademark reply does not have to be the same as my dad's. But it should at least as powerful.

Before my teenage years, whenever asked how I was doing, I learned from my dad's leadership and developed my own response. Without anyone prompting me, I would respond, "I am rich and happy."

If you can choose a unique, powerful trademark response to this common question, you have the mental discipline to do what Brian Tracy calls "mastering the mundane." Select a new life response. When someone asks you about how you are doing, make the decision to use your voice and personality to spread gross national happiness.

I heard someone else respond to the question by answering, "If I would be doing any better, vitamins would have to take me." You are enrolled in the H.A.R.V.A.R.D. Effect. As a graduate of this curriculum, your biggest responsibility is to use your supernatural resources to astonish the world with value.

Get creative. When you open your mouth, you tell the world who you are. *How are you?* That short phrase can lead to an infinite impression. This question is asked of us more than any other question during our lives, yet so many of us waste the opportunity. You won't. You will seize the moment with every encounter.

Here are ten ways that you, as a H.A.R.V.A.R.D. Effect Graduate, should never respond to the world's most asked question:

- Fine.
- Good.
- Great.
- Awesome.
- I've been better.

- Hanging in there.
- Alright.
- I've been better.
- Tired.
- Amazing

Don't allow your mind to be colonized by these typical responses. Your mind and body hear everything you say. No single person's happiness matters more than our collective gross national happiness. Let us not waste our moment of self-disclosure.

This assignment challenges you to create a scripted response that can do two things, identify your highest version of happiness, and inspire a stranger to feel better about themselves. Just for meeting you. If they dare to ask a generic question, will you dare to astonish them with a maximum positioning statement?

Some of the happiest people I've ever met were people who had been diagnosed with mental disabilities. Early in my music career, it was very tough to get anyone to believe that a motivational speaker would produce any songs in hip-hop that people would like. The first person to give me an opportunity was a producer named Levon Davis, whom I have always called. LD-4.

LD-4 was a musician who knew how to play a variety of instruments. We spent countless hours in his studio. I patiently waited while he would produced original instrumentals from scratch. During the day, LD-4 and his wife worked at a non-profit organization, called ARC, which stands for Activities for Retarded Children.

The name stood out to me, because my father had been labeled "retarded" as a child. I thought a good way for me to give back was to volunteer at ARC. I thought I was going there to give back, but, after a few hours of meeting the kids and adults who were there, I realized the gift that they were giving me was much more than I could imagine.

There was Craig, Jimmy, and my closest friend, Jeanie. Jimmy was a lively spirit. Down Syndrome prevented him from being able to tie his shoes, but it did not stop him from tying a bow of happiness around his life. Jimmy was an incredible bowler. He even had a job that he maintained and loved.

Jeanie would come in early in the mornings, and, when she would enter I would say, "Hello, Jeanie, how are you doing?" But it was more important to Jeanie to remember to put away her jacket in the closet, so, sometimes, my return response would not come for 10 or 15 minutes. When her tasks were complete, and she was able to process my question, Jeanie's smile would light up my soul. After volunteering for ARC and being hired to teach there for a year, I got a chance to get a world-class education in happiness.

We have nothing to complain about. If we have been blessed with all our mental faculties, we must remember not to take them for granted. I got a chance to interact with happy parents who have loved their children through the both the worst and best of times.
If I had not known the students at ARC, I think I would have felt too much shame to ever share my voice like I did at my Grandmother's funeral. Sometimes, we get devastating news. No matter what you are going through or what someone might say about you, *you* own your mind. Even if it has been labeled different, it's *yours*. *Never* be ashamed of your intellectual property. *Never* shy away from your biggest idea of what your life can be.

When people ask you how you are doing, give them the same smile that Jeanie gave me after she finished putting away her jacket. Come up with a response that is more powerful than every negative thing that has ever been said about you.

There is no excuse big enough for you to hide behind. Your truth can be something that makes an infinite impression, even if you must be vulnerable. Don't you dare stop being astonishing.

Maximize Your Downtime

The second resource that we must manage is the often-untamable beast that mankind has labeled time. Tick tock. The time is ticking. Beep, beep, the alarm is buzzing. Outside of our calendars and devices, time is something that we can control. You have complete dominion over your mind, and you *must* manage the power that you have to transcend hours and days and weeks.

There is an old Cherokee saying that reminds us, "Either you run the day, or the day will run you." One time, after a speaking tour, my father returned to his master bedroom in our high-rise condo on the Southside of Chicago, to find a devastating note from his baby boy, I wrote him a letter that asked one simple question. "What does it profit a man to gain the whole world and lose his youngest son?"

No matter the calling on our lives, we must, somehow, find a way to do more with less time. In addition to running a multi-million-dollar enterprise and meeting the demands of the marketplace, I wanted to remind my dad that, as a resource manager, I needed him to manage to fit more time in his schedule for me.

When you are a high-achiever, downtime is a very limited commodity. Balancing hard work and healthy family is, perhaps, the most difficult juggling act that any go-getter can ever learn. If there was a way for me to teach you how to turn 24 hours into 100 hours, I would. I can't even guarantee you that applying the principles of resource management will make you feel less overwhelmed.

What I *can* tell you is this. Your downtime, the time when you are not in your office or on your campus. The time when you are not in a meeting or spending time with your family. I mean the time when it's just you. The time when no obligation needs to be addressed. That is called downtime.

I learned about downtime at an early age. Even though I was getting bad grades and I knew it, the report cards had not come home yet, so I knew my parents were unaware of my lack of focus. When I was placed on what was called "room arrest" before my grades were known, my dream life became a nightmare.

When you live in a three-story mansion, being stuck in the house is too much fun. I was placed on room arrest. I was permitted two food breaks and two bathroom breaks. The keyboard from my computer was removed, and my screensaver became a haunting reminder of the torture of no digital outlet. To top it all off, in addition to not being able to watch television, the door of my room was removed, eliminating the thought of privacy.

When I asked my warden— I mean my dad— why he put me on punishment, his answer surpassed my understanding. I said, "Did you talk to my teachers?" He shook his head with a smile on his face and said, "No."

"Well, did you see my report card somehow?" I thought maybe he had paid somebody to get an early draft or something. I wasn't sure, but I had to figure out who the snitch was that got me placed on room arrest.

He looked at me with a straight face. As a matter of fact, it was almost as if he was looking through me, and he said, "I'm putting you on room arrest, because of how you are using your downtime."

Enough said. The rat was my downtime. The problem was, I had never heard of downtime before that moment. On room arrest—unable to talk on the phone, watch television, or surf the Internet—I had a lot of time to think.

I began to try to define downtime. He could have said, "I'm putting you on punishment, because of how you use your time." Now, that is something I could have easily understood. But, what my dad was teaching me was a lesson that every child does not learn at an early age. As I sat in my room, staring at where my door had once been, I started to understand that not all time is the same.

For the sake of this semester, I don't want you to look at your time with a homogeneous eye. Let us dissect this mystery by using different name qualifiers for the different types of time. Horizontal time is when our bodies are laid flat. Most of us call it sleeping. However, that neglects to take into consideration how important horizontal time is for the body. Without a certain number of hours of rest, as supernatural as our minds may be, they begin to glitch.

Then, there is vertical time. This is when our bodies are not resting, but upright. The time when we do whatever it takes to climb the ladder of competition. Many people complain that their vertical time is stressful and overwhelming. Many auction off their vertical time to the highest bidder, even if it is at the cost of their happiness.

We will focus in on our downtime. As I sat, trapped in a room without doors on the hinges, I began to contemplate the true meaning of downtime. I blamed her for my unhappiness. Downtime ratted me out and took away my recreational freedom. I had never heard of her before. Still, I was determined to learn more about her, so that she didn't snitch on me in the future.

That is when I learned the true essence of why they call it downtime. In my arrogant opinion, downtime is the most precious form of time that we have at our disposal. The reason why they call it *down*time is because that is the time when most people engage in the activities that prevent them from going *up* in life.

According to the Bureau of Labor Statistics, the average American—ages 15 and older—has approximately five hours of leisure time a day. I know we have been trained to think of our day's as having 24 hours to get things done, but, the truth is, after the time we
spend horizontally sleeping and allowing our bodies to recuperate, and the time we spend vertically, in motion and climbing the mountain of achievement, there are only five hours left for us all. To be exact, it's five hours and five minutes.

Maybe that is why we complain about time running out, but so many of us walk when we chase it. Just last night, I received a text from a very talented close friend.

Sarah said, "On paper, my life is going well, but I am exhausted and feel like I'm drowning." Of course, I offered her some encouraging words, but I wanted to tell her that I could relate to how she was feeling.

305 Minutes to Drown

Surprisingly enough, Sarah was not calling me from a swimming pool, nor the beach. As a matter of fact, she had just got a promotion at her job. Yet, despite ascending to triumph on paper, she had a little bit of downtime to text me how she, like so many of us, feels on a regular basis. Some people answer the question of how they are doing by saying, "I'm just trying to keep my head above water." That doesn't mean that they are having a tough time learning how to swim. Downtime, after your job or school is over, when you're not sleeping and you have five hours and five minutes to use as you please, the last thing you want to do is feel like you're drowning. Drowning is one of the world's universal fears.

Even if you do know how to swim, depending on the distance that you're swimming, exhaustion can lead to drowning. That is why we have what are wisely called *lifeguards*. When I was on room arrest, I felt just like Sarah felt when she sent me that text. Everything looked good on paper: I was one of the top youth speakers in the industry, we had moved from a condo in Chicago to living in a mansion in Potomac, Maryland, and I was attending the best school possible, yet I was still drowning in my own mediocrity. I needed a lifeguard.

My dad put me on punishment before he knew I was failing any of my classes, because he knew that a lifeguard can only do the job correctly if they move at the right time. It is a life-or-death type of urgency. I responded to Sarah as though I was a self-improvement lifeguard. I knew she was being vulnerable. I blew my whistle and dove in motivational first, before she got too much water in her lungs.

I responded, "You were born with a life vest made of willpower. Recharge, and remember that you are on a quest. Once realized, you'll be drowning in worthiness. Not busyness."

At the time that I responded with that text, I thought all drowning was the same. I just figured that, if she was drowning anyway, maybe I could remind her that she was drowning in something that was worthwhile. I did my best to convey that.

Freshwater and saltwater creates a very different drowning effect. 90 percent of drowning does not take place in an ocean. The salt water of the ocean cultivates a different experience altogether. So, what is the main difference between salt-water drowning and a freshwater drowning? You guessed it. Time.

In fresh water, because the structure of the water is like the structure of our blood, drowning takes place in two to three minutes. That means a lifeguard has a very small window to do his or her job. Different from the police officer or the fireman, the lifeguard has the smallest window of time available to become a hero.

Although the ocean has colossal waves and the potential for sharks in dangerous territories, the saltwater of the ocean—which is very different from the structure of our blood—dramatically delays drowning. Salt water extends the window of rescue from two to three minutes to eight to ten minutes.

Don't allow your downtime to become your drown time. I understand that you are very busy. I know you have built a very high demand for your attention. You were born to be happy. Don't sink your 305 minutes of daily downtime. It is yours to do with how you please.

I am only going to ask you to give five minutes of it each week to the H.A.R.V.A.R.D. Effect. The rest is yours, as it should be. The more things you include in your downtime agenda, the more exhausted you will be during your other times of operation. Be it horizontal or vertical, however, if you can find some saltwater to wade in, a lifeguard might just get to you in the nick of time.

If you ever get too overwhelmed and begin to feel like instead of living the H.A.R.V.A.R.D. Effect, you are stuck in The DROWNING Effect. Remember this: maximize your downtime.

In Gary Keller's book, *The One Thing*, we are reminded that "The people who achieve extraordinary results, don't achieve them by working more hours, they achieve them by getting more done in the hours they work." I would like for you to achieve more in the hours when you are not working. I want you to keep in mind that being busy is not an acceptable excuse for including new effective time-bending habits into your arsenal of doing.

Part of the challenge we must all face is the fact that, when we are at the top of our game, the demand for our time increases dramatically. It leaves even the most gifted among us swamped in calls, or drowning in emails and business cards.

When your horizontal, vertical, and downtime is occupied, and someone calls you, if you don't answer the phone, they are instructed to leave a voicemail for you. It can be a chore to check messages when you are moving and shaking. I must admit, sometimes, when I'm on a speaking tour, if people keep calling me, my voicemail will tell them that, "The voice mailbox is full," and ask them to please call back later. This is the worst possible outcome. I want you to get in the habit of maximizing your downtime, by capitalizing on your voicemail power. What are the three most effective things a person could do in their downtime?

    1) Enhance their communication skills.
    2) Empower their souls.
    3) Encourage others from afar.

By harnessing the effect of voicemail power, you can do all three in under five minutes, allowing the remaining five hours of downtime to remain unoccupied. Your next assignment will require you to change your cellphone voicemail on a weekly basis. I want you to remember that all the people who are working for your time may not get it. You might not answer every phone call, but that doesn't mean that you cannot inspire every caller. Shifting the perspective about your voice message and allocating just five uninterrupted minutes a week to changing it, sounds like an easy task. Let me share with you why it is not.

In the late 1870s, Thomas Edison announced his invention called the phonograph. This was the first recording device invented that could play back sound. Over one hundred years later, during the late 1970s, the phonograph technology that allowed Earl Nightingale to record his album and that allows callers to leave a message when we are busy, became accessible to anyone with a phone.

We have not been leaving voicemails for very long. You would be disappointed to learn that the first words ever recorded and played back by Edison were, "Mary had a little lamb." Whenever someone calls you, and you don't answer, nowadays, people can take it as an insult, even if it's not personal. Have you ever sent a caller to voicemail, just because your time to talk was limited? It happens to the best of us. I want you to maximize your downtime to leave a voicemail that is so powerful that callers hope you don't answer the phone.

Why is that? If you can make your voicemail message so unique and powerful, that every time you miss a call, people will thank you for not missing an opportunity to use your voice for good. How would that affect your life, if you never allowed the fact that someone couldn't reach you to be a reason not to truly reach out and touch their hearts with something special?

Most people's voicemail is very basic, just like "Mary had a little lamb"—not much thought is put into it. Even worse, the same voicemail can be stuck on a person's machine for years. Part of avoiding resource mismanagement is not only updating your mental software, but also updating your voiceware.

September 10, 2001, the First Family of Motivation made a television appearance. The next day, I was scheduled to fly from Miami back to Los Angeles. My dad and sister were scheduled to catch later flights.

When I left that morning, I didn't want to wake them, so I took a few moments out of my downtime to write a little letter saying how much I loved them, and goodbye.

I had no idea that the very same day, terrorists would highjack airplanes, and there would be a grounding of all flights. My plane had an emergency landing in Dallas. I was 17 years old, and I was informed that the Twin Towers had been attacked, and that there was no way to catch a flight out. So, at 17, I was stranded in Dallas, Texas. I didn't know what to do, nor who to call for help. The first time I called my dad, I got his voicemail.

This was a gift. He was never the type to waste the phonograph technology by recording a weak voicemail. He regularly updated his message service to inspire others, even when he was busy. If you've ever heard any of his motivational audios, just imagine the ones he made for his friends and family who were trying to reach him when he was unavailable.

It was a national emergency. The world was drowning in fear. But, when I heard that message of hope in his voicemail, it inspired me not to panic. Just long enough for a lifeguard to come to my rescue.

In your downtime, do your best to be a lifeguard. Take the time to leave a powerful weekly voicemail. Every time someone calls you and gets an answering machine, it will be a call that answers the questions that they might have about life. Something that has the potential to help people to stay afloat a little bit longer.

Eventually, I received a call from someone who worked for the minister T.D. Jakes. I was no longer stranded. The Jakes family sent someone to pick me up from the airport, and they gave me a place to stay until air travel was allowed again. During this time, I would hear one of Bishop Jakes's most powerful statements; "Some people can breathe off the oxygen of your attention."

If you pay a little more attention to your voicemail in your downtime, there's no telling how many more people's oxygen you can help maximize. I am forever grateful to the Jakes family for looking after me during that time of global crisis.

I'm also grateful for my dad's voicemail. I'm happy he didn't just say, "Mary had a little lamb, leave a message after the beep." The oxygen I gained when I heard his short motivational voice message reminded me to be strong. I had two lifeguards on September 11th. Your job is to be a lifeguard every day by changing your voicemail once a week in your downtime.

Can you do that? If so, you are on your way to becoming an optimal resource manager. It will force you to research powerful quotes that you can insert in your voicemail. Also, your recorded message will sharpen your communication axe as they improve in quality and as you get more creative and passionate with your delivery.

You never know who's drowning when they reach out to you. Maximize your downtime by looking at your voicemail as an opportunity to be a lifeguard when callers are unable to reach the oxygen of your attention.

Raise Your Relationship Capital

Perhaps the most challenging supernatural resource at our disposal to manage is the resource of relationship. High-earners get a lot of traffic in the relationship lane of life. I have learned that mismanaged relationships are, at times, more costly than mismanaged finances.

According to *Forbes*, 96 percent of startup businesses fail within 10 years. I would dare to say that 96 percent of startup relationships, most likely, fail within that same period. The most effective resource managers look at themselves as relationship-preneurs.

The main reason most businesses fail and people stop printing out their business cards that once excited them is that most businesses are undercapitalized. It takes capital to make money. Just like it takes relationship capital to make the things happen that money cannot purchase.

When managing your relationship capital, I want you to begin to look at the people in your life in three unique ways. You don't just have friends, associates, and colleagues. When you look at your life as a relationship-preneur, you should categorize your relationships as shareholders, stakeholders, and placeholders.

I remember it like it was yesterday. I was in a super-teaching session at CEO Space International when it clicked for me. Berny Dhorman was speaking about the new rules for raising capital for a startup business. Up to that point, I had only learned about earning money — I had never known it was possible to raise it, and I definitely didn't know how.

I decided to update my mental software and learn the foreign language of capital, just as you will learn how to become fluent in multiple languages of relationship capital. When dealing with a relationship that is with a potential shareholder, there is a process that has proven to be successful.

You can't talk to a shareholder the same way you would a placeholder. Nor can we address the stakeholders in our lives in the same manner that we address our shareholders. The ability to communicate and understand the language of relationship capital can remove barriers that create exceptions to the rules.

A shareholder in business is someone who is solely interested in the big ROI, which as you know stands for Return On Investment. Free market enterprise is built on the cornerstone of ROI. When you have a lot of money in the bank, the problem is, it's not growing if it's still in the bank. Smart, accredited investors look for shares of stock that can reap multiple earnings. Once an entity has undergone a capital valuation to determine what price to allow for shared ownership, an outsider can own a piece of a company that they know very little about and that they put in no actual sweat equity in building. It allows people to earn more money off their shares of stock than they could have ever made if that same money was complacently stuck in their bank accounts.

The moment that their shares start to devalue, many shareholders will sell their shares of ownership to the highest bidder. Keep in mind that every soul you share your life with will own a part of you. The experiences that you create with each other, the bonds that you form in friendship, love or business, must be properly valuated.

If entrepreneurs can determine what a company is worth, relationship-preneurs should be able to determine what a connection is worth. Cash is the oxygen of a business. Collaboration is the cash of relationship.

You can identify your relationship portfolio by calculating a potential collaboration the same way an auditor calculates a company's stock. The word "resource" is defined as a stock or supply of money, materials, staff, and other assets that can be drawn on by a person or organization to function effectively. Managing the assets of your mind, your time, and your relationships is essential to fulfilling dynasty.

The word "dynasty" originated from the I Ching and describes the "origin of the universe" or a "primal force." If we look at the primal force that is has created all that is not manmade, we can quickly observe that competition is a false threat. The forests do not compete with the oceans. The mountains do not fight against the air.

The origins of the universe and the primal forces that enable us to live and thrive are rooted in collaboration. Competition is not a natural resource. It is manmade. Through the power of relationship capital, we can align our supernatural resources with the ultimate primal force.

I know what you're thinking, *What is the ultimate primal force?* The answer is undisputed. The ultimate primal force is collaboration. The wealth of collaboration is derived from relationship capital.

In business, everyone cherishes shareholders. Shareholders are willing to invest their money with you. They are willing to risk money for a better return on investment. Shareholders can get the initials of your company onto Wall Street, but they cannot land your family on the runway of dynasty.

Don't get me wrong, shareholders are great. These are people who are willing to invest the time that it takes to share their life with you. They believe that having you in their life will reap a sizable ROI. Therefore, shareholders are good to have, but they will not last in your life, without making some type of withdrawal. You see, the shareholder relationship is one that is based on competition and withdrawals. A stakeholder is a relationship that is based off collaboration and deposits.

The moment a shareholder does not see adequate returns on investing time and energy with you, the relationship's capital decreases, and you will no longer become a priority in their life. It is important not to take this personally. A shareholder is only interested in your success, if your success adds to their bottom line.

Many people who enter the shark tank of entrepreneurship never learn the main reason why no one wants to invest in their big idea. They tell people about it and, sometimes, develop extensive business plans to illustrate the idea, but fail to effectively manage the resources that they have to capture the momentum that is required to take their idea to where it needs to be.

Begin to look at yourself as a relationship-preneur. The business of your life can grow a lot faster and serve more people when you see yourself that way. There are some people you were born to meet. There are some friendships that will magnetically charge you up. But, when we look back at our lives, after decades of introductions to strangers, there are only a few relationships that last the test of time. The great networkers of our time are constantly swamped by business cards that they will never follow up on. We must pick and choose who we will invest the 305 minutes of downtime each of us have daily.

I decided to start spending more time with people who knew how to raise money.

That meant that none of the people who were in my life at the time would be qualified shareholders of my downtime. Some of them were funny, some of my relationships were exciting, but none of them knew about raising capital. If they *did* know about it and didn't tell me, I would have been furious. This capital-raising phenomenon was the most exciting concept I had heard of in my life.

I did whatever I had to do to invest in CEO Space and attend every conference I could. There, I met people who had raised millions of dollars. Berny Dhorman, the man who first awakened my interest with his audio, *Super Rush Seed Capital*, was once, himself, called the Billion-Dollar Man, because he raised over a billion dollars for different businesses in various industries.

One day, I was heading toward the front row of a workshop Mr. Dhorman would be teaching. It was at a beautiful resort in Henderson, Nevada. The air reeked of royalty and prosperity. As I walked into the conference room to get my front row seat, I suddenly felt the strangest push from behind. It felt like a foot had kicked my butt.

I instantly turned around with an attitude to see what happened. I couldn't believe it when I saw Mr. Dhorman return his foot to the floor and say with a straight face, "I had to kick your behind, for not being my son." I was honored. Ever since then, I refer to him as my other dad. He updated my mental software and building up the relationship capital with him as a shareholder has totally shifted my paradigm.

My dad's first major shareholder was a teacher by the name of Leroy Washington. Leroy Washington was the teacher that my dad mentions in all his speeches. One day, young Leslie was in a different classroom to visit one of his friends. Mr. Washington mistook him for his twin brother, Wesley, and asked Leslie to solve the problem on the board.

Leslie told Mr. Washington, "I can't do that, sir." Mr. Washington said, "Why not?"

The other children in the room started shouting "He's DT, he's DT." Mr. Washington was confused by the outburst and silenced the room.

He looked at young Leslie and said, "Why are they calling you DT?"

Leslie said, "You're mistaking me for my twin brother, Wesley. I'm, Leslie and they call me that because it stands for the dumb twin. I don't belong in your classroom, sir, because I'm educable mentally retarded."

On that day, my dad got his first major shareholder. He would use all his downtime he could studying Mr. Washington and learning from him, even though he was not one of his students. Mr. Washington looked at my dad and gave him the seed capital he needed to catapult him away from special ed.

He said, "Don't you ever say that again. Someone's opinion of you does not have to become your reality." Mr. Washington withdrew the best out of a little adopted boy, who never got a chance to meet his father. Mr. Washington became a father figure who expected a greater return on investment from him than he ever expected from himself.

Berny Dohrman became my Leroy Washington, and, no matter how great you are as a leader in your industry, unless you properly recognize the shareholders, stakeholders, and placeholders in your life, you'll never succeed as a relationship-preneur. Failing to succeed as a relationship-preneur makes it nearly impossible to be an effective resource manager.

Now, before we distinguish the difference between shareholders, stakeholders, and placeholders, let us talk about how to treat potential shareholders. You definitely don't want to scare them away, and, trust me, they don't wear a sign around their necks identifying themselves. But, occasionally, you'll be introduced to someone, and it will feel as if your spirits have a kindred connection.

Keep in mind, in business, people are competing for customers. In school, people are competing for grades. In life, you are competing for relationships.

People who form profitable relationships maintain a durable competitive advantage over relationships that have no value exchange.

Don't miss a moment to connect with a shareholder. They want to attach themselves to the stock of you and share the rewards of your acquaintance. Make sure that you keep it in perspective when you meet new people to share your life with. They were not put in your life to care about you. They were not put in your life just to shake your hand or take a selfie with you. Some people that you meet will see your dynasty. Some relationships you form you recognize the power of your hundred-year plan, and there will be parts of that plan that they will see how they can benefit from that.

Just don't be surprised if some of the shareholders of your time and attention abandon the relationship the moment they can't see what they can get out of it. That is why so many startup relationship-preneurs never form relationships that last over ten years. We forget that shareholders are only interested in ROI. If it takes too long to give them that return, they will invest their relationship capital with one of your competitors.

If you want relationships that are not defined by circumstance or net worth, what you are really looking for is a stakeholder. The difference between a shareholder and a stakeholder is quite dramatic. A shareholder is focused on return on investment. The moment they can invest their time and energy in a more profitable relationship, they won't need you anymore. A stakeholder is focused on COI, cost of inaction. These are the peoplewho are not just involved in reviewing the stock, but are concerned about the overall performance of *you*. Return n investment asks, *What am I gaining from this person?* Cost of inaction asks, *If I don't take action and give to this person, how can they be at their best?*

To truly maintain a shareholder relationship, it requires you to be valuable. To acquire and maintain stakeholder partnerships, it requires us to be coachable. One of the biggest stakeholders in my life is a man by the name of Farrah Grey. One day at a small L.A. health food restaurant, my dad and I were sitting at a table, and I was the first to notice the best-selling author of *Reallionaire* walk through the door. I had seen him on TV many times and was honored to be in his presence.

To my surprise, he approached our table and greeted my father by saying, "Mr. Les Brown, when I was a child, my mother would sit me in front of the television and make me watch your show. Great to meet you." My relationship-preneur instincts kicked in, and I quickly learned why people have been calling him a "reallionaire" since the age of 14.

A millionaire is someone who is usually known for making millions of dollars over a period of time. A *reallionaire* is someone who *really* has millions of dollars in the bank all the time.

Farrah Gray grew up in the projects in Chicago, a city that has been called Chiraq—a play on words Chicago and Iraq—because more devastating murders have taken place in that city in recent years than there have been committed during the entire Iraq War. But brother Farrah had a mother who groomed him into a powerful resource manager.

Before he was ten years old, he began selling painted rocks door to door in his neighborhood. He took pieces of cardboard and cut out and designed his own business cards, since he could not afford professional ones.

Imagine how resourceful you must be to think of that while other kids are thinking about video games.

He began using that cardboard business card as a stock to grow his relationship capital. On it read the slogan, "The 21st Century CEO." He used this slogan to update his mental software, so that saw himself as more than a person who was living in poverty. His environment was not the leader of his happiness.

He used his downtime after school was over and his homework was finished to sell painted rocks, since he could not afford any other products to sale. One day, he gave his cardboard business card to a man named Roi Tauber. Roi Tauber gave him something most people who live in the slums of our nation never get a chance to experience. That experience is what I call relationship capital.

At eight years old, Roy Tauber would become Farrah's first stakeholder. He invited Farrah Gray to a think tank and suggested that he start a business club with some like-minded youth.

Roy didn't have to do that. He could have just taken the little kid's card and kept going about his day. But he saw in Farrah what Farrah saw in himself, and he must have asked himself this question, *What will it cost the world if I don't act on his behalf to help him be even better than he is now?* Fortunately, little Farrah was coachable and started a business club. He called it UNEEC, which stood for the Urban Network Economic Enterprise Club.

The relationship capital from this UNEEC club increased, until it attracted the attention of shareholders who were interested in investing in their ideas to profit off them. By the age of 14, Far Out Foods, an idea from the think tank to sell syrup, had done over 1.5 million dollars in sales. When he eventually sold that company for millions, he didn't want to call himself a millionaire. He started seeing himself as a reallionaire. I knew that as a relationship-preneur, I needed to have more people in my life who could call themselves reallionaires.

I asked Mr. Gray, who had been born in the same year that I was born, "What projects are you working on now?" The answer was astonishing. We were both 25 years old, I had never met someone so accomplished at such an early age.

Then, he told me that one of the things he likes to do in addition to his various philanthropic projects is to buy and sell money. You heard me correctly. He buys and sells money. I couldn't believe it. I never knew there was an industry. He went to the car and came back with a thousand-dollar bill. A bill that was issued in 1934 and is worth a lot more today.

Ever since that day, we stayed in touch. Stakeholders are the ones who inspire you to do more than you can imagine, because they are already doing it. They don't need anything else from you than for you to better yourself. You can have great transactions with shareholders, but you will have great transformations with stakeholders.

Carl Jung wrote, "The meeting of two personalities is like the contact of two chemical substances: if there is any reaction, both are transformed." I would call on my dear friend and mentor Farrah for a favor that would totally transform my relationship with the future. When I asked Farrah Gray to be the godfather for my son—the Leroy Washington in his life, the Berny Dhorman in his ear—he accepted. I instantly knew he didn't take the role lightly and is truly committed to ensuring Mamie Brown's dynasty.

The first thing he did was ask for a picture and posted it to his 360,000 followers on Instagram with the caption, "My godson, Honor Brown, this little boy is bound for glory and greatness, he has my vote in 2049." By the way, both Honor Brown and Farrah Gray were born on September 9th.

The relationship capital I leave for my son will be worth more than anything that is in my will. I am choosing to position my life in a way that, if he had an emergency landing in any city, there would be a trusted stakeholder to look after him. I agree with Oprah Winfrey when she said, "Lots of people want to ride with you in the limo, but what you want is someone who will take the bus with you when the limo breaks down."

Shareholders might be there for you when you need them. Stakeholders are there for you before you know you need them. Placeholders are there for you when they need you, but we'll dive into that a little later in the chapter.

I want you to ask yourself, if you were a relationship-preneur and you valued the relationships you currently have in your life, how many shareholders do you have? How many stakeholders are you in contact with? The number of shareholders will always be higher than the number of stakeholders, and that is okay. It is important to be able to distinguish between the two to properly deal with them.

If you mistake one for the other, it can cost you relationship capital that you cannot afford to lose. When communicating with shareholders, don't take it personal. What do I mean by that? Don't take it personal if they're not in love with your dynasty. Don't take it personal if they want to withdraw from you everything they can from the relationship. That is why they saved your name in their phone.

Nowadays, we have lost touch with what it means to be a friend. According to data from the General Social Survey (GSS), the number of Americans who say they have no close friends has roughly tripled in recent decades. When people were asked how many confidants they have, "zero" was the most common response.

If you have zero stakeholders in your portfolio, your relationship capital is severely depleted. It is not entirely your fault. Keep in mind most relationships are competitive. That means that, as you meet new people, you must compete against all the new and old people they have met, to make a lasting impression.

A relationship-preneur never backs down from competition, but they realize it's immaturity. Confidants or stakeholders are harder to come by, because they use the primal force of collaboration as their growth mechanism. I once heard Bob Proctor say, "If a business isn't growing, it's dying." The same applies for relationships.

Several scientific studies reveal powerful facts about relationships and how they impact our health more than smoking cigarettes or exercise. I began to ask, *How many positive relationships can a person have at one time in their life?*

That is when I learned about the Dumbar number. In the 1990s, British anthropologist Robin Dumbar found a correlation between brain size and average social group size. By measuring the size of the neocortex part of the brain, Dr. Dumbar proposes that humans can comfortably maintain 150 stable relationships. The Dumbar number teaches us that there are cognitive limits to the number of people with whom one can maintain stable social relationships.

Facebook has a 5,000-friend limit. In the real world the number is only three percent of 5,000. That is still a lot of relationship capital potential. We meet thousands of people in our lives, but, when it comes to close relationships, we seldom keep track of the number. Unless you realize that part of your most profitable skillset as a resource manager is to be a relationship-preneur. To be a relationship-preneur, you must understand that social isolation is the new bankruptcy.

Phobia vs Philia

A person who lives to 80 years will usually at least encounter 80,000 people. But, according to the Dumbar number, the shares of relationship capital are limited to 150 units. If you have 10 or 20 units of friends, you are not winning as a relationship-preneur. In fact, you are barely scraping the surface of your relationship capital potential.

Out of all the 80,000 or so people you meet in a lifetime, you must pick and choose which 150 people are going to be in your portfolio. I have developed a mathematical formula that allows you to use your estimation skills to calculate your exact relationship capital number.

As you earn the trust of more shareholders and stakeholders, your relationship capital number will grow. When you are selecting which people you choose to share your life with, keep in mind that, ultimately, you with have the capacity to keep less than half of one-half of a percent in your life.

Put yourestimation cap on, because once you complete this exercise you will have an assumed value of your gross relationship capital. Aristotle was right when he said, "No one would choose to live without friends, even if he had all the other goods." Think about all your friends. Begin to make a list of them. How many do you have? That is a question only you can answer.

Estimate the total of how many friends and relationships you have. Let's abbreviate relationship capital for the sake of our formula. Relationship capital = RC.

Whenever dealing with variables, I remember using x and y as symbols that can represent different values. In this formula, $x=$ Age and $y=$ number of friends.

If I've lost you already, please bear with me. Multiply your age by 1,000. Divide that by the difference between the Dumbar number and the total amount of all your relationships in your life.

This formula will produce a number that represents your RC. $RC= \{1000x / 150-y\}$.

In the online course for this book, there will be clear instructions on how to use this RC number to determine a perceived value for each of the three types of relationships you have in your life. The value of our dynasty will boil down to the power of our relationships.

To be a resource manager, you must manage your mind, your time, and your relationships. Rethink your duties in these three areas, and keep in mind that philia always overpowers phobia. Many of our modern ideas stem from historical relationships that few are aware of. "Philia," which means fondness or abnormal love for a specified thing, is the one thing that stands between us and meaningful relationships.

Let's face it, we live in a time of networker overload. Just because we meet someone new—whether a prospect or potential friend—doesn't mean that you will have philia for them.

As a matter of fact, most people do not excel as great relationship-preneurs, because they develop a phobia about relationships. What if someone lets you down? What if one of your relationships lie to your face or behind your back? How much time out of my life is this new relationship going to cost me?

On May 27, 427 BC, Aristocles was born. The boy's father was rumored to be related to the ancient kings of Athens. But Aristocles would never have the privilege of learning from his father, Ariston, because he died while Aristocles was still a boy.

Aristocles was known as a quick-witted young man. When his mother remarried, he had access to the best teachers in Athens. He was also very athletic and became a young wrestling champion. There, his wrestling coach gave him a new alias. He became known as Platon, meaning "broad," because of his broad shoulders. This man developed relationship capital that would keep his dynasty alive for over 2,500 years.

Think about the power of your relationships as we look closely at the relationship capital of the man who is known as the inventor of philosophy. Way before Isaac Newton and Albert Einstein, or Earl Nightingale or Les Brown, there was Aristocles, who became known to us all as Plato.

Plato met a young mathematician named Pythagoras. If you're a fan of math, you might have heard of the Pythagorean Theorem. This formula in math deals with measuring of the relationships between three sides of a triangle. Our Relationship Theorem deals with measuring the equity of our relationships.

It is a known fact that Pythagoras inspired Plato, even before young Plato met the wild revolutionary known to the world as Socrates. After learning from the best teachers of Greece and meeting Pythagoras and Aristotle, Plato's relationship capital began to soar. Influences like these inspired him to open what was called The Athens Academy. The Athens Academy in Greece became their Harvard University. The philosophies that developed there gave birth to Western Civilization's common sense.

Socrates was seen as a revolutionary, because he asked the wrong people the right questions, and it rubbed the right people the wrong way. He inspired people to think for themselves, and he developed a relationship with the young minds of Athens. Even though they had no wealth or political power, the political elite eventually started to see him as a threat.

Their nation was at war with Sparta, and they felt like it was dangerous to keep a man around who forced people to question power, the gods, and democracy, as a whole. Socrates was sentenced to death after a public trial and a vote. He was charged with corrupting the youth. Socrates was forced to drink poison. Plato loved him too much to witness his final day on earth.

Plato had met him for the first time when he was 21 years old. Socrates, himself, never authored any works, but Plato was a stakeholder in his vision for the future. Many had heard of Socrates in Athens. But only one person, Plato, formed an academy that was rooted in his teachings. There, he argued that the rulers of tomorrow should be the philosophy kings. He invented the sport of philosophy.

Plato used the Socratic method (named after Socrates) to invent philosophy and logic. The Socratic method is "a form of cooperative argumentative dialogue between individuals, based on asking and answering questions to stimulate critical thinking and to draw out ideas and underlying presumptions." Advocating for men and women to use their minds to come to their own definition of fulfillment.

Socrates had no idea that his questions would initiate a relationship with a student who would train another student by the name of Aristotle. Because of the relationship capital between Socrates and Plato, and the relationship between Plato and his best student, Aristotle, the world of philosophy has transformed the hearts and minds of men and women for generations.

Anais Nin said, "Each friend represents a world in us, a world possibly not born until they arrive, and it is only by this meeting that a new world is born." I would not have a career today, were it not for Plato's master student, Aristotle, and Aristotle's master student,

Socrates. Aristotle literally wrote the book on rhetoric. A book that is known among scholars as the most important book that has ever been written on the art of persuasion.

There is a timeless way to dramatically increase the value of your relationship capital and overcome any phobia you may have about being a full-time relationship-preneur. Aristotle taught us about it, and it's called *philia*. Aristotle describes the activity of *philia* as, "The wanting for someone what one thinks good, for his sake and not for one's own, and being inclined, so far as one can, to do such things for him." This is the ultimate characteristic of a stakeholder relationship.

On the journey of dynasty, you will encounter people who want the best for you. I know we are raised not to talk to strangers at an early age, but every stranger you meet is not working against you. Some strangers will become allies in your hundred-year plan, and you might not even recognize the influence you have on them.

Western ideals were born out of the relationship capital formed by those three intellectual giants centuries ago. The right kind of shareholder relationships are on their way to you.

A new face that it might be easy to overlook. Let new relationships open a new world within you. It may be hard to believe while we're living in a jaded world, but remember this quote by Frederick Buechner, "You can kiss your family and friends good-bye and put miles between you, but at the same time you carry them with you in your heart, your mind, your stomach, because you do not just live in a world but a world lives in you."

There is a world that lives in you. When we accept someone into the trust of our attention, keep in mind the reason they want your attention in the first place is to open the door to the world that comes with it. Your attention is special. Part of the most difficult task of being a resource manager is choosing who *not* to spend your time with. Let's face it, in your whole life, if the average person meets at least 80,000 people — don't you want to choose the best 150 out of that 80,000?

It is important to seek out the environments that are going to have the best value for our future's future. Unfortunately, everyone you meet will not be stakeholder or a shareholder. Our job is to distinguish between them and address them, according to the value they have been assigned from our relationship capital number.

Develop a standard procedure about how you will deal with shareholders. Think of all the ideas you can to properly honor and address a stakeholder.

Last, but not least, we must address the relationships that are the least, but the most plentiful. What will be the standard protocol that you use when you encounter placeholders?

People who become the best in their field are often criticized about how they treat those who have not attained the same heights. Why is that? How can one seem so nice and pleasant on TV or in pictures, but treat people so mean if they appear to have nothing to offer them?

In my opinion, the more you achieve, the more people fight for your attention. The more people who are attracted to you, the more you will interact with placeholders. What are placeholders? Placeholders are people who have learned how to pull you down, but they can never lift you up.

The worst thing one can do as a relationship-preneur is to mistake a stakeholder or shareholder for a placeholder. I made this mistake with my brothers and sisters. Being the youngest of 11, I guess you can say I was born with more RC than the average baby.

Calvin is my oldest brother and the CEO of our family company. If you ever get to meet a no-nonsense person who doesn't believe in beating around the bush, you know my big brother. He is the master of saying no to placeholders. That is why he is the CEO.

Serena, my oldest sister, manages the family fortune. Even when we were children, she was the only one of my siblings who paid just as much attention to the receipt after a good meal as she did to the menu.

Patrick, my second oldest brother, has the biggest heart in the world. After our father was diagnosed with prostate cancer, he decided to become a home health aid, so that if he ever had to take care of dad, he would be prepared. We call Patrick Mr. Integrity. I'll never forget all the childhood functions that my dad was too busy to attend, but not

Patrick. Regardless of where he or I was in the world, whether it was a basketball game or a sixth grade graduation, Patrick was there. He is dependable, and now works as our road manager.

Ona, my eldest sister, is an inspiration. Outside of making the Harvard event happen and being a master negotiator, Ona is a highly sought after speaker in her own right, and I am her biggest fan. Sometimes, it can be challenging growing up in the shadows of greatness. Ona makes it look easy.

Tia, my most organized and structured sister, is in charge of all strategic planning. Last but not least, my sister, Sumaya. Sumaya is very short, even in high heels. But, give her a pen to write, and she becomes an intellectual giant. She is the best writer in the family and reviews all our bodies of work.

This is just half of the relationship capital I was born with. As a child, I always thought I was competing against my siblings. That made me look at my brothers and sisters as just that. Now, as a grown up, I have learned that they are not just placeholders in my life. I have become the man I am today because of their love and thoughtfulness. Sure, I have other brothers and sisters. However, this core group has taught me a priceless lesson. You are not alone.

There might be some placeholders on your dynasty journey. That is to be expected. Some people might not see anything more than a human being when they look at you. I tell you this now. If you don't remove the placeholders from your life, you'll never make the room for the people who can help you grow.

I had to come to a place in myself where I didn't just look and my brothers and sisters as relatives. I realized that some of my friends that I liked to have fun with were never going to help stretch me to the next level. Some relationships are dead weight, but my brothers and sisters are some of the biggest stakeholders in my life, and, every time we do anything great, I'm reminded how rich I am in relationship capital to have them in my lives.

Recently, our dad endured a back injury that made it difficult for him to walk and caused excruciating pain throughout his back and leg. All the stakeholders in my family came together to support our vibrant hero while he was reduced to giving his speeches from a wheelchair.

Have you ever seen the person you look up to suffer? As positive as we all are, it takes a toll on you. Together, the Brown family must manage our relationship capital and make sure that our father's time and energy are not wasted on placeholders. After 40 years of changing lives *for* us, now, he must change lives *with* us. As he enters his mid-70s, we must see his body of work as our classroom of intention.

We are all committed to spreading our dad's story and message beyond his life. We look at him the same way Plato looked at Socrates. The same way Aristotle looked at Plato. He is a master professor.

The task of following in our dad's shoes may be too epic for one soul to strive for. But, together, as one, our relationship capital amongst ourselves can never die. Because of our love. Because we have a vested interest in this world, even after the last living Brown has taken their breath. Our dad—that young twin boy, Leslie—he is immortal. The truth that burns in his heart also brands ours. We are fully committed to managing our family resources in a way that honors him. The best resource managers influence others to manage their resources on their behalf, even after their lifespan is complete.

To achieve this daunting objective, we must always examine our three major supernatural resources: Our minds, our time, and our relationships.

VIRTUALIZE YOURSELF

*"Most people are awaiting virtual reality.
I'm awaiting virtuous reality."*

- Eli Khamarov

Welcome to your senior year in the H.A.R.V.A.R.D. Effect. I hope you are proud of your progress and ready to act on the most critical assignment thus far. By now, you have learned that the dynasty curriculum is engineered to challenge you to reimagine, inspire, and innovate your way to the top of the global ladder.

In a borderless economy, I have personally seen a rapid transition like no other. Just one generation ago, a person could be successful if they worked hard and surrounded themselves with a few powerful influencers. Today, the bar has been astronomically raised.

When I was a child, sending someone a text message involved going to the post office and purchasing a book of stamps. Come back home and write out the message. Place that message inside of an envelope with the address written on the outside, and stick it inside of a mailbox. Then, we had to wait for someone to come and pick it up, without having a specific idea about when they would receive it.

One time, my sister, Sumaya, came in town with her choir, and I wanted to surprise her and just show up. The problem was, I wasn't quite sure what church to show up to. I had to go in this antiquated thing called the Yellow Pages and call every church in a certain area.

Let's face it. In the most recent decades, we've moved from local businesses that were built on brick and mortar to global conglomerates that are fueled by click-and-order. A periscope used to be something that a kid could use to look at the stars. Now, Periscope is an app that can be used to become a star. Being a senior in the H.A.R.V.A.R.D. Effect comes with more perks, but there is greater responsibility.

The Worldwide Learning Curve

What happens when everyone in our global village must learn something new? I'll tell you what happens. The non-learners become non-earners. Analog thinkers won't thrive in a digital age. It is important to recognize that, to ensure the long-term sustainability that dynasty requires, we must be well-versed in the latest technological advantages.

Therefore, your senior assignment is to embark on a virtualization experiment. If a tree falls in a forest on an island, and there's no one around to hear it, does it make a sound? This question possesses a unique conundrum for mankind. I would like to pose another question that is rooted in a similar principal. If a life ends and never makes a mark online, can it make a long-term difference?

In 1710, the philosopher George Berkeley was trying to find out if something can exist without being perceived. Well, a lot has changed since then, and, in 2017, the motivator John-Leslie Brown wants to find out, *Can something powerful be perceived, without being virtualized?*

The answer to both questions is no. *Scientific American* answered this question from a strictly physical point of view. They wrote, "Sound is vibration, transmitted to our senses through the mechanism of the ear, and recognized as sound only at our nerve centers. The falling of the tree or any other disturbance will produce vibration of the air. If there be no ears to hear, there will be no sound." [5]

Your life is also a vibration. In the real world, the vibration of your air must end.

Within the virtual world, your vibration of the Internet can be infinite. This is the first time in human history in which a person can be anywhere—and everywhere—all the time. As my mentor, Farrah Gray, would say, "Visibility is just as important as ability." All the abilities of the world are now victim of the digital divide. Without the ability to master the emerging technologies, one's entire life can be removed permanently, if it never makes a sound on the island of the Internet.

The main ingredient of immortality is not to be bitten by a vampire. Nor is it to be blessed with superpowers or to be immune to all diseases. The secret ingredient to immortality is to actualize a virtual dynasty.

My Uncle Boo never got a chance to go on YouTube or to watch his best friend from elementary school, my dad, influence up to a million people a day online. His real name was Alexander Whyms. When he and my dad met in the second grade, my dad didn't know that was he going to become the world's leading voice in personal development, nor did young Leslie had no idea that his friend, Alexander, would be a stakeholder in his dynasty.

I can recall the story I heard about when my dad cashed his first million-dollar check. Sure, the money was great. But the feeling of throwing 100k up in the air in a hotel room and swimming around in it like thirsty fish with your best friend from elementary school was priceless.

My mother gave me my middle name, Alexander, after the man who I have always known as Uncle Boo. Please don't ask me why. Still to this day, if you ask anyone in our family who the best cook was, they will tell you, without hesitation, Our Uncle Boo.

Unfortunately, Uncle Boo passed away when I was a teenager. He didn't write his own obituary, but I would have loved to have heard it. I know he would have loved to see me give that speech at Harvard.

At his funeral, a stranger made a statement about his life that I will never forget. On our way out of the church, where his going-home celebration was being held, I was standing next to my dad on one of the saddest days of his life, and a woman came up to him and asked, "Hey, Les, sorry for your loss. But did Boo ever make that coo book you always talked to him about making with all his secret recipes?" While holding back the tears, my dad said, "No. He didn't." She said with the sadness of a person who never digested a home-cooked meal with love, "Oh, I'm sorry to hear that he took that with him."

I will never forget that day. Nor will I forget the conversation I had with myself after eavesdropping on theirs. I told myself that day that, when I die, I don't want to take anything with me. I'm going to leave something behind that showcases the best parts of me.

Since the time of my uncle's death, a lot has changed. The global learning curve has balanced the playing field and changed the rules of the game.

Rule number one: if you don't learn how to upload your greatness and build a community around it, it's as if your greatness does not exist. The digital divide makes some people feel like the Internet is for hobbies. Maybe to binge watch their favorite TV show or do a little shopping. But, while running for office, I met a young man named Jim Gilliam, who told me to watch his video on YouTube called "The Internet Is My Religion."

Jim Gilliam is the CEO of a company called NationBuilder. This company offers the world's first platform for leaders, handcrafted from scratch to help you grow a community and lead them to action. NationBuilder is the one-stop-shop for anyone running for office. Whether managing voter profiles in your area or accepting donations online, Jim Gilliam and his team of young, fearless, and casually dressed geniuses can help you launch, grow, and win a local, state, or national campaign. That is why, after meeting this very tall, bald, strange-looking man, I couldn't wait to pull out my phone and watch his video. What did he mean by that? The Internet is his religion? That is a tad extreme, don't you think?

It started out with him talking about the three pillars of a global movement. According to Jim Gilliam, those pillars are stories, tools, and faith. Keep in mind, I am a very harsh critic when it comes to speakers. But, by the time I finished watching this this 12:27 second video, I would never look at the virtual world the same way again.

Jim's father had worked for IBM, and, when he brought home a funny-looking phone and plugged it into his computer, 12-year-old Jim had two main loves in his life: attending the church that was across the street from their home in Silicon Valley and surfing the Net. At 12 years old, he would communicate with people of all ages ethnicities and backgrounds. They had no idea he was a 12-year-old. Jim was an introvert in person, but, online, he was an intellectual. In his own words, he said, "I was judged by my brain, not discounted by my age."

By the time Jim was in college, the Internet had grown exponentially. Did you know that, in the past 15 years, alone, the number of Internet users has increased from 738 million in 2000 to 3.2 billion in 2015? Well, Jim was always at the cutting edge of that growth. While in college, he stayed in the computer lab, like Napoleon Hill used to stay with his pistol. As a matter of fact, he even spearheaded the project of bringing the Internet to Liberty University's campus.

Suddenly, Jim Gilliam was walking on campus like he always does, and he felt like he was drowning. He couldn't breathe. When he was rushed to the hospital, something happened that rocked his faith at the core. He was diagnosed with a lethal form of lung cancer called Non-Hodgkin's lymphoma. If you thought that was bad enough, his mother was diagnosed with cancer as well and passed away soon after. Jim's faith was shattered.

It wasn't until he learned of an experimental procedure performed by UCLA that he began to hope again. He needed two brand-new lungs to stay alive. Unfortunately, his hope was snatched from him when UCLA rejected him from their program because of the difficulty of the surgery. Once again, Jim's faith was ravaged by the realities of life and certain death.

So, Mr. Gilliam did what all techy, introverted genius' do when they have a life-defining moment: he blogged about it. Suddenly, UCLA began receiving emails, accusing them of inflating their stats by rejecting each case that appeared to be too difficult.

Suddenly, people from around the world who had never shook Jim's hand, nor looked him in the eye, began to lobby UCLA and swarm them with emails. Jim had no idea that one blog could do more for him than thousands of prayers. But it did, because, one morning, UCLA called his phone and informed him that he had made it onto the list that he had previously been denied from.

The Internet is not my religion. But I understand where this young computer scientist is coming from. You see, without the power of community that the Internet affords us, there is a plethora of global relationship capital that we miss out on. That blog about UCLA ended up saving Jim's life. Now, imagine if Jim had never written that blog? NationBuilder. The platform he has built for grassroots leaders of all types—he would have taken that with him.

A hundred years from now, NationBuilder will still be a profitable entity. This semester will remind you that the Internet is not a hobby factory for you. When you graduate from the H.A.R.V.A.R.D. Effect, you will not have the luxury of looking at your browser as some type of retail outlet or never-ending entertainment vortex. The Web is here to connect us, not just comfort us. Do you think we went from wooden chips to silicon computer chips, just so we wouldn't miss the latest episodes of our TV shows? You are a part of a new effect now that understands fully that, when you share your life with the world, the world will not hold back what it shares with you.

For Jim Gilliam, it was a set of lungs. Now, I have a question for you. How do you know if you need to undergo a virtualization? The correct answer is this: if you have lungs. If you have lungs, you must take the worldwide learning curve seriously.

Today, the world's top doctor is not Dr. Oz, nor even Ben Carson. The world's top doctor is a college dropout by the name of Dr. Google. More people go to that website in one hour than will ever visit any one hospital.

The first computers communicated with each other on October 29, 1969. The same hospital that saved Jim Gilliam's life, also brought to life the movement that has become the Internet. There were no Macs or Microsoft computers then. Robert Taylor and Larry Roberts innovated on Ada Lovelace's dynasty and sent the first message from UCLA to Stanford University.

Here is the first thing you should know about your upcoming assignment: when you virtualize yourself, you don't have to be great online to get started, but you *do* have to get started online to become great.

Thousands of years before the invention of the smartphone, homing pigeons were the fastest form of communication. I became curious about how these pigeons were trained. Often, ministers and motivators can draw inspiration from the mighty bald eagle. Think like an eagle, not a pigeon, people say. But the eagle never communicated on behalf of a leader. The pigeon has gotten a bad reputation over the years, despite its irreplaceable contribution to how humans send messages across long distances.

I'm here to tell you something that might seem disturbing, if you haven't done your research. When it comes to virtualizing yourself, don't try to be a bald eagle, think like a homing pigeon. Build a nation online, and allow that nation to lead you beyond the limits of the physical world.

To train a homing pigeon, there is a process. We will use this same process to retrain ourselves to view the Internet as more than a convenience. But what if you are not a celebrity or building some type of business? What can you do with the Internet, and why should you? Isn't there enough noise online? Why should you add something to this technological ensemble of chaos? I've been there. I've had those same thoughts. Jim Gilliam already answered those questions for us.

You don't have to be an aspiring pop star, nor some egotistical life coach to build a nation online. All you need is a pair of lungs—and a good Wi-Fi connection, of course.

Now, remember this heirloom from the Brown dynasty. You don't have to be great to get started, but you must get started to become great.

When they sent that first message from a computer at UCLA to one at Stanford, they did not send a smiley face emoji, nor some type of memorable historical quote. They had the other party on the telephone and, first, they just sent one letter: the letter *L*.

Then, they asked, do you see that? They said yes. Then, they sent the letter *O* and said do you see that? They said, "Yes, we see the L and the O." Then, they sent the letter *G*, and the entire system crashed. In October of 1969, three letters were virtualized, and it crashed the best technology that existed at the time. Even though the systems crashed, one of the men who were in the room is quoted as saying, "Then, the system crashed, but, yet, a revolution was born.

This revolution has created a worldwide learning curve, and, to master it, we must think like the pigeon. A homing pigeon must be trained with three primary learning tools: a home, a secondary home, and hunger.

The funny thing is, as a child of parents who were never married, I kinda always had a home and a secondary home. In fact, my dad has built a career around telling people that they must be hungry to achieve success. With a hungry, trained pigeon, you can send a message up to 100 miles.

When you introduce the homing pigeon to its base of operations, you must persuade them with food. Then, you physically take that pigeon to the secondary home a few times and make sure that it eats well. By the time you take that same pigeon back home, remove all the food. This makes the pigeon hungry.

Before I finish the story, let me impress this upon you: to virtualize yourself today and build a digital estate plan for your dynasty, you gotta be hungry, like the homing pigeon. Sure, eagles can always soar higher than pigeons, but no one can ever accuse them of being hungrier than a pigeon. I rest my case.

When the pigeon is let out of the cage at the first home, where there must be a way for the pigeon to get back in without getting out, the pigeon will leave the first home and fly directly to where it has learned that there is another source of food. After it is done eating, it will return home again, and repeat the same routine.

Think like a homing pigeon. You have two homes now. Why do you have two homes? They both will feed your dynasty. Your physical home and your virtual home. My job is to make you hungry. So hungry that you soar online like a pigeon and spread your message with the digital world.

Is it going to be easy? No. Why not? Because of the learning curve. Nowadays, there's a new social media site popping up every 15 seconds. How do you avoid getting overwhelmed by the spammers of the world and build a virtual nation around your life story in a way that leaves the Internet better than you found it?

Once again, I repeat, the Internet is *not* my religion. But I *do* have faith in the Internet. I have faith in our global village. Now, we need the stories and tools to transform our short lives into sustainable virtual value.

More people have learned more from Dr. King after his death than they could have possibly done when he was alive. We could never touch him again. But time and time again, his dynamic spirit and compassionate tone touches our hearts. This one man's voice becomes more influential as each decade passes by. You, too, will be influential beyond your life expectancy.

When you graduate from this curriculum, your dynasty will be assassination-proof. Prison-proof. Economy-proof. The insights here are timeless and relevant.

The first thing you must do is where many people get discouraged. I promise you, it's not as hard as it sounds. The first way to virtualize yourself is to turn your body of work into a blog.

Once upon a time, there was a learning curve, called reading and writing. If you learned that, it was a big deal. Now, digital literacy is just as important. No matter what your age or education level, you are capable of blogging.

What would you blog about? How would you set it up? Who would want to read it? Those questions are no longer relevant. That's like telling someone that they need to learn how to read and write and hearing them respond by asking, "What would I read about?" Or, "How would I get a book?"

Before you count yourself out, let us learn a little more about learning, itself, by asking this quintessential question: how long does it take to learn something new? Some say 10,000 hours. As a matter of fact, a student named Josh Kaufman asked that very question after having a newborn baby girl. He realized that his downtime was very limited, so he began to research exactly how much time it takes.

He came across a study that was borrowed by Malcolm Gladwell in his book, *Outliers*. In *Outliers*, Mr. Gladwell shows the work of a professor who studied athletes and top performers and concluded that it takes a minimum of 10,000 hours to learn how to perform at expert capacity. 10,000 hours is equivalent to five years give or take a few weekends off. Unfortunately, with a newborn baby, a new marriage, and a full-time job, Josh didn't have an extra 10,000 hours to spare.

Deeper research lead him to conclude that, although it might take 10,000 hours of practice to learn how to become an expert, becoming an amateur at something and learning how to do it efficiently only requires 20 hours of practice.

Now you know. It only takes 20 hours to learn something new. Do you think you can manage that? Putting 20 hours aside to virtualize yourself. No more, no less.

I know how overwhelming it can be. At first, I didn't understand the virtual universe. I thought that it was a distraction from real life. I was wrong. Sure, there are a lot of questionable things about the power of virtualizing for one's life. Paramount on that list is the freedom of privacy.

The truth about the matter is this: if you don't make your presence on Earth known online, when your presence leaves this earth, all of you is gone forever.

Your blog is going to be about your hundred-year plan. Your blog will be about the past that you love that will enable others to live better in the future. Your digital imprint will become your permanent footprint on society.

Did you know that the Internet was not made for celebrities? It was not meant to be an endless gossip column. The Internet was invented to balance the learning curve, by providing all the information known to man available to any man or woman at the push of a button.

Borderless Wikinomics

Take a company like Wikipedia, for example. When they announced that their goal was to give an encyclopedia to everyone on earth for free, how do you think the people at Encyclopedia Britannica felt? To this day, the encyclopedia books cost over $1,300. Thanks to the virtual world, the founder of Wikipedia, Jimmy Wales, and a group of dedicated volunteers could imagine a world where every single person on the planet would be given free access to the sum of all human knowledge. With one employee, Wikipedia is a nonprofit run purely on digital donations.

Up until the virtual revolution, the encyclopedia was the best archive of all human knowledge. There was just one problem. All humans did not contribute knowledge to those volumes of all human knowledge. What makes Wikipedia so revolutionary is that anyone with lungs can contribute to Wikipedia. Anyone with lungs and a Wi-Fi connection can add input and expertise to the history books.

Reporters would ask, "Mr. Wales, won't it be digital chaos if anyone can contribute?" Surprisingly, no. Wikipedia is one of the top ten websites worldwide. With one employee and millions of contributors. They don't have to charge people a dime. They provide so much value online that they don't need to have a physical office. The digital capital of community is priceless in this day and age.

I am proud to say that one of my stakeholder cousins, Kam Talbert, has taught me the biggest lesson I have learned about virtualizing myself. Through Kam's good friend and A-list actor Joseph Gordon-Levitt, I have personally and professionally profited from something that is called Wikinomics.

What is Wikinomics? Well, you are going to learn what it is firsthand. We are going to use Wikinomics to complete the rest of this book. Let me dive deeper.

One day, my cousin, Kam, who is a super-talented actor and singer told me about this cool new virtual playground. Turns out, Joseph's brother and him created an online production company that allows everyone and anyone to contribute. If any of these major productions become profitable, they participate in the profits.

One day, Kam invited me to a HitRecord event at the historic Orpheum venue in Hollywood. I ended up sitting directly next to Joseph's grandmother. He opened the show by acknowledging her dynasty. The energy in the room was electric. All these people, who had only met virtually, were under one roof. Many people were in the audience, but I was the only one sitting next to Joseph's grandmother. His Mamie Brown. It reminded me of the power of relationship capital.

But Joseph had broken the Dunbar rule. He managed to have relationships with thousands of people through HitRecord. He's collaborated with people whose hands he has never shook. He put money in pockets of people who live hundreds of miles away. Here's the catch. Joseph is already a celebrity. Why would he need to virtualize himself even more? What did he know about the virtual world that I didn't?

I decided that I was going to ask him his secret. I wanted to know what made him think so differently and come up with HitRecord. At the after party, I said, "Hey Joe, great event. Tell me, what are you reading?" He looked at me and smiled. I instantly knew that none of his other buddies had asked that question. He answered with a recommendation that I could not have anticipated. He said, "*Wikinomics*, by Don Tapscott."

Don Tapscott learned about Wikinomics from his neighbor. Don's neighbor was a banker who had recently purchased a gold mine. The problem was, none of his expert geologists could determine where the gold was. Don's neighbor almost gave up. He decided to try a virtual experiment before he called it quits.

Usually, gold mine owners keep all their geological findings in security-protected supercomputers that very few people ever have access to. He decided to go against the grain and publish all his top-secret data online. He offered a $500,000 cash prize for anyone who could tell him where the gold was. This virtual experiment paid off big-time. It wasn't one of the world's top geologists who found the gold. It was a 3D mapping company who made a virtual map of it. Don Tapscott's neighbor discovered 3.2 billion dollars' worth of gold that he would not have known was there, were it not for Wikinomics.

Economics would say that you are crazy to publish your geological findings. Wikinomics says that you are crazy *not* to. A million eyes are better than two. That is when Mr. Tapscott coined this term that Joseph adopted to help thousands of people earn thousands of dollars that they would not have earned, without working together as a team. According to the author, Wikinomics is what happens when you harness the power of mass collaboration.

There was a time when we were taught that we had talent inside of us. Now, we must learn how to match that with all the talent outside of us. Only then can we truly learn the power we unleash when we virtualize ourselves.

Your senior project will demonstrate the power of Wikinomics. Apply the assignments from each semester and blog about it. Email your blog to johnlesliebrown@harvardeffect.com. The submissions from each participant that completes the assignment will be used in the final print edition of this book. Each time someone enrolls in the H.A.R.V.A.R.D. Effect coaching program, it results in profits that the contributors will participate in.

As you read the books, if you have any questions or ideas, share them with me on this live Google document.

Most people would ask the question, *What if someone takes the book down or uses your ideas for the book?* That's a question *economics* would ask. A *Wikinomics*-thinker asks. How can the readers of this book make the book better with their ideas?

Better yet, *How can they benefit from the book financially, outside of applying the action steps in their lives?* Ultimately, we can hold each other accountable for the application of this book. With your help, we can join the best doers list.

Success doesn't come by it reaching the bestsellers list, it is discovered by reaching the best doers list. Apply all the action steps listed in this book, and improve upon them. Take things out. Put new ideas in. Send us your blog—either written or video—and your story can become a chapter that inspires generation after generation. I'm publishing the geological specs, because I know that there is a 3D mapping company that can add to this and improve it. From Aug 1, 2016 to January 1, 2017, join our private Facebook group and share your journey with our community of high-achievers. By Feb 17, 2017, we will send out signed copies to all preorder participants and contributors. Everyone is encouraged to write one chapter about their experience. That chapter is called "Acknowledge Your Journey."

Before we get there, let me help you overcome this learning curve. You have four months to spend twenty hours on The H.A.R.V.A.R.D. Effect. At least three times each week, I ask that you post within our private Facebook community about your journey. All the content that is liked and shared the most within our community will be used in the book. Here is the big difference-maker: those who participate in the writing of the book will also participate in the profits of the book, or donate them to charity. Half of all profits made from the book sales, album sales, and coaching sales will be distributed amongst the best doers whose stories and transformation will be added to this volume of the book.

Each quarter, starting in the first quarter of 2017, a profit update video and profit-sharing list will be added to the Facebook group and www.HarvardEffect.com members-only area. Economics says that profits need privacy. Wikinomics knows that transparency is the new gold.

To participate in this virtual experiment and receive payments for your contribution to the book, you can start by registering at HitRecord.org to familiarize yourself with this revolutionary model. On Dec 1, 2016, more details will be revealed.

The Social Credibility Movement

For this book to really effect your life, I need you to help me get what is needed to be a true world-class difference-maker. That doesn't come by giving one speech at one school. It comes by seeing the results in people's lives. I have a lot of major relationship capital. Usually, when there is a product launch of this magnitude, you must use something called borrowed credibility. Borrowed credibility used to get people's attention. The virtual world has presented us with a new form of credibility that cannot be borrowed. It can only be earned.

By applying these principles into your life, and sharing them in our private Facebook group, you will be helping me build social credibility. Let's face it. Presently, I only have about 1,000 followers online. None of my YouTube videos have ever received one million views. We live in a time in which low social media numbers means less opportunity. Less people impacted by my message. I plan to change that. However, Gary Vaynerchuck and Seth Godlin remind me that small is the new big. I'm grateful for each and every like, heart, or follower I can get online. But I have more to share with the world than what I ate for lunch today.

Even when I am no longer around, I want my son, Honor, to be able to pull out his phone and brag about how powerful and viral his dad is. That can only help, if this body of work truly makes a difference in your life and the lives of your family. Together, we can build a dynasty. Further instructions will be given with our private Facebook community. Thank you for reading part one of the H.A.R.V.A.R.D. Effect.

Part 2

Immediately after making this book available for pre-order, all my questions were answered. Is it possible to have a book that is not one-sided? What happens when the readers, themselves, are enrolled in the writing of the book?

The first participant was a woman by the name of Renée. Renée never had a great relationship with her mother, but her memaw, as she calls her, became her Mamie Brown. Keep in mind that Ms. Renée works at a restaurant called the Olive Garden, where, between working 12-hour shifts, she decided to invest in herself by pre-ordering *The H.A.R.V.A.R.D. Effect*.

Renée has had the least amount of time and fewest resources, but, somehow, she has contributed more to the H.A.R.V.A.R.D. Effect than even I could. She has given it social credibility. I asked for her help. I asked for her to rewrite the book. Edit it. Add your ideas. She took time out of her busy schedule to do just that.

Borrowed credibility will always keep you chasing someone or something that you think you need. When people get degrees, they get to borrow the credibility of the institution they graduated from. However, since I didn't graduate from a fancy institution and neither did Renée, we must depend on social credibility to earn our respect. Renée contributed and rewrote the first 60 pages. On her own time and dime.

With just one Renée, this theory has transformed from a monologue to a dialogue. I would rather judge the success of this book, not by how many copies I sell, but by how many Ms. Renées who read this stop working in restaurants and start owning them. In the middle of working on the logistics of a Wikinomics miracle, my mentors began to tell me the truth about how they felt about the title of this book.

Keep in mind that this is my first literary baby. I have chosen this title and these topics for a specific reason. But certain expert confidants tell me that it can limit my reach, due to the competitive nature of the Ivy League. All of the Princetons, Yales, and Stanfords of the world may take offense to the title and never open their ears or doors to hear my message. Think of all the borrowed credibility that I would be missing out on.

This is precisely the reason why it is important to virtualize yourself. This entire book project, and all the concepts within it, could have been stuck on some Microsoft Word document, somewhere where only I could read it. We all have those types of projects that we work very hard on, but never allow to see the light of day, because of the credibility question.

Who will be interested? What if nobody watches my video? My big concern was not just that, but what if no one had any input? What if everyone read the book, but nobody made a hundred-year plan? What if everyone read the book and created their plan, but nobody's plan came true? How would we ever know? Thank infinite intelligence for the Renées of the world and the Wi-Fi connection.

Renée has made this book special. So has Jessica Noe, Timothy Thomas, and Steve Yuzenco. One of the things that everyone always says about the Internet, is that once you put something online, it's there forever. Even if you backspace or delete it, there is still some digital DNA left in the Cloud. To the powers that be who don't think it is a good decision to release this book, tell that to Renée, Steve, Jessica, or Amanda, all of whom have uploaded videos online about how this effect has impacted their daily life. Sure, I will do the smart thing and rely on borrowed credibility to get sales with my next book, *It's Your Time*, but *The H.A.R.V.A.R.D. Effect* is not about that. It's not about doing what sells, it's about doing what's next.

When you apply the strategies in this book, you are operating with the most advanced curriculum. By not relying on old thinking, it will set a new standard. When these few good men and women virtualized themselves by reading the book and sharing their insights, they made this body of work immortal. Because of your big voices, these small pages will live forever. Thank you for giving me social credibility.

Nowadays, there is a whole new generation of high-achievers who face a whole new set of challenges. For instance, how do we teach our children and our children's children not to make online choices that have offline consequences?

We must teach them that the virtual playground is unavoidable. There will be bullies and nonsense. We cannot just sit them in front of a browser and tell them to start searching. It is a new responsibility, but we must urge the next generation of digital natives to serve as virtual architects for an innovative tomorrow.

Will you become a virtual architect with me? Will you use the Internet to spread hope and methods, or will you use it to spread gossip and trauma? Some people go online to watch fights. Others go online to fight for a better world. Unfortunately, some people still choose to live offline, not fully understanding that what is left offline is left out of forever.

There are several mental hurdles we must leap over to earn social credibility. Number one: it cannot be purchased. Anyone can buy digital credibility.

The main benefit of virtualizing yourself is to monetize your products. I am not urging you to be a digital marketer; I'm urging you to be a digital messenger.

According to the Chief Marketing Officer Council, digital advertising will continue to be the fastest-growing market segment over the next five years, with projected compound annual increases of 12.7 percent. The only problem is, people don't just go online to be marketed to.

Marketing gets in the way of what we want to see. The question is: what do we want to see? Less marketing, more mesmerizing. Less information, more substance. More authenticity, less persuasion.

Unlimited community is the harvest for a virtualized life. It's not about just using Hootsuite to post on all the distribution channels. It's not about looking at your email list and examining how many people click on your link. That is not why the Web was formed. No human was born a digital marketer. The Internet was born to turn the big world into a room. Its purpose is not to turn the big world into a little cash register.

I urge you to become a digital messenger. One day, all the digital marketers will grow old and weak. Their fancy homes will remain, because digital marketers keep a percentage of what they help others make online. Yes, they will live the good live if they have a high conversion rate, but they leave no legacy beyond what they have earned. A digital messenger is a profession that is not profit-driven. A digital messenger has social credibility, and, even after their death, their names will remain relevant.

When your life story goes online, it never has an ending. You can control your immortal impact. Don't let some marketing plan interfere with the power and precision of your intuition. If you never get a million followers online, you are not a failure. However, if you cannot be a part of a worthy community, you have yet to scrape the surface of modern success.

Forget the picket fence and decent-paying job with benefits. Forget leaving your family behind for a paycheck. If you virtualize yourself and take full responsibility for building or joining an online community, you will never have to be delayed by distance. Do it now. The worldwide learning curve requires this. In the following chapter I will lay down the foundation for your new digital messenger career path.

Your last virtual experiment involves your cellphone and the number two search engine in the world. YouTube is one huge search engine. I am looking for 1,000 digital messengers to launch a YouTube channel to share stories of hope and strategies of high-achievers. Will you participate in this process?

YouTube is only 12 years old, but I guarantee it will be around a hundred years from now. And so will your YouTube channel. More people upload content to YouTube in 60 days, than the top three major television networks ever produce in 60 years. This allows for social credibility to trump the power of gatekeepers. YouTube is the new gate, and you can use it for free. Something you put on YouTube at 12 can dramatically impact the opportunities that are available to you at age 21. So let us be strategic and positive. Not just comical or critical. Use your experience and expertise to make an undeniable digital contribution.

As we near the conclusion of this semester, don't forget that the most challenging part of virtualizing yourself is the length of the learning curve. You can never stop learning. We must be in a constant state of discomfort. The good news is that you don't have to carry that burden alone. The whole world must learn how to use tools that haven't been used by previous generations of thought leaders.

I would have loved to see Albert Einstein's YouTube channel. However, it is because of Newton, Lovelace, Einstein's immortal impact that a YouTube channel is able to exist.

Don't just do it for me; do it for all the fallen soldiers of truth who never got a chance to exercise their digital privilege. Many poor resource managers will tell you they lack the desire or ime to exercise their digital privilege. But, imagine, if you will, the digital footprint that Abraham Lincoln would have made, if he knew that such a thing as Twitter could exist. Picture the inspiration that would have live-streamed from Mahatma Gandhi's Snapchat. The digital privilege was possible even way back then, but society did not even know it.

I believe that the iconic world-class communicators of yesterday would have been even more influential today. It took a worldwide learning curve to discover the science of the virtual economy. Make it count. For the thought leaders who will never know what Google is.

Your three senior virtual experiments are as follows:
- Make a blog.
- Become a digital messenger and create a positive YouTube

channel.
- Create your own Wikipedia page.

The history books that exist today come to life without pages inside of them. Add your name to the pageless history book. The power of your story will not end when your life does. If you don't graduate from these experiments, immortality will always be impossible for your dynasty.

ACKNOWLEDGE YOUR JOURNEY

*"Every day is a journey, and
the journey itself is home."*
-Matsuo Basho

Congratulations. You have earned your bachelor's degree from the

H.A.R.V.A.R.D. Effect. I never thought I was intelligent enough to get into Harvard. Now, I am smart enough to know that when you utilize the same principals and harness the power of emotional intelligence, you can develop a scholarly approach to achievement.

The sad part about the long road of achievement is that, sometimes, your biggest victories will have no witnesses. Unless you are a celebrity or have a major following online via virtualizing yourself consistently, your life's championship will never get a press release.

Ribbon Recognition

A woman by the name of Helice Sparky Bridges is the founder of Difference Makers International and has developed a global reputation as the First Lady of Acknowledgement.

Every school must have a graduation ceremony at the end of the lesson. Why is that? They understand how to use the power of acknowledgement. It is that power of acknowledgment that motivates students to become scholars. You might have once believed that you lacked the knowledge needed to live life in a class of your own.

We are in a shift from a knowledge-driven economy to an *acknowledge-driven economy*.

Over forty years ago, Mrs. Sparky, The First Lady of Acknowledgment decided to launch a campaign that has touched the lives of over forty million people. She entered communities and taught them how to conduct a blue-ribbon ceremony.

Before she reached over forty million people, it all started in one classroom. Mrs. Sparky equipped one teacher with her infamous who-I-am-matters ribbon. The teacher then acknowledged each individual in front of the class and explained why she cared about them and celebrated their contribution. Each student was given three additional blue ribbons to give to people outside the classroom who they wanted to acknowledge.

Let's pause there. Look at what Mrs. Sparky ignited. This teaches us the first law of an acknowledge- driven economy. You see acknowledgement is a double-edged sword. Not only does it affect you by receiving it, but, if you can learn how to give it to others, it can become a lethal weapon of achievement.

Ms. Sparky learned that 42 percent of kids are bullied on the Internet. She did not just listen to that statistic and say, "Oh, that's such a shame." She did something about it. She unleashed a weapon of mass acknowledgement in the form of a blue ribbon.

When the kids from that first class went out into the world, Mrs. Sparky could not have known that one of those kids would give a blue ribbon to a corporate executive. He acknowledged him for being a great career mentor and giving him career and school advice.

He left the executive with the other two ribbons. That exec then gave it to his boss, who was known for being grouchy and rude. But he acknowledged him as a creative genius and left him with the final blue ribbon. That night, on the way home, the boss of the company was wondering who was worthy of the blue ribbon.

He decided to give it to his son. He got home and said, "My days are really hectic, and, when I come home, I don't pay a lot of attention to you. Sometimes, I scream at you for not getting good enough grades in school or for your bedroom being a mess. But, somehow, tonight, I just wanted to sit here and, well, just let you know that you *do* make a difference to me. Besides your mother, you are the most important person in my life. You're a great kid, and I love you!"

The boy starting crying. It was the first time the boy had ever felt loved by his father. All from one blue ribbon. From one bold woman. 40 million ribbons later, the rest is dynasty.

The boy could not control his tears. The father went back to work the next day and told the young executive that his son showed him a gun last night. He had planned on committing suicide, because he felt unloved. That one little blue ribbon saved his son's life.

Now is the time for you to acknowledge your journey. The fact is, we can waste a lot of time being too busy to notice the power of acknowledgement.

Sometimes, after your plan has been made and you have followed through on your worthy ideas, you must figure out a way to give yourself a blue ribbon.

Celebrities and athletes have extravagant award shows to be acknowledged for their abilities. You might not ever win a Tony or an Emmy, but you can't get the competitive edge if you don't acknowledge your journey for who you are and what you've been through.

In a knowledge-driven economy, if you are smart enough, you succeed the most. Yet, studies from the NBA reveal an unbelievable connection between the number of acknowledgement bumps, as I like to call them, and the number of overall victories.

If you have ever seen an NBA basketball game, you have seen a multitude of acknowledgement bumps and probably didn't recognize their hidden power. Let me paint a picture for you: The Cleveland Cavaliers are playing the Golden State Warriors. Lebron James goes up for a layup and gets fouled. Immediately, three of his team mates come over to him and give him a high five or a back slap, even if he misses the shot. They are using acknowledgement bumps.

Lebron walks to the free throw line. He is one of the best players in the world, and he literally gets a free uncontested open shot. He shoots and makes it. All his teammates come and acknowledge his shot. Every one of them. High fives and good jobs. Whoever wins the game, you are sure to see a huge acknowledgement bump in the form of two chests jumping into the air and colliding in celebration.

The University of California took eight months to study all the acknowledgement bumps that take place during professional games. In a 48-minute basketball game, a whole minute and a half is spent giving positive feedback. The NBA was surprised to learn the results from Michael W. Kraus and his team, who discovered that the teams who high-fived the most at the beginning of the season win more games by the end of the season.

Don't wait until the end of your season or the end of the game to start celebrating you victories. When you are looking to score in life, remember that your life is a journey.

There might not be four living souls to high five you or fist bump you every time you get fouled in life and still manage to come up with a way to score. This semester will give you the motivation to fist bump yourself, even when nobody is around.

The first rule of the acknowledgement-based economy is simple. Knowledge is a sword, but acknowledgement is a double-edged sword. The standards of greatness have less to do with how smart you are and more to do with how often you are willing to acknowledge the power within you and the people around you.

The second rule of the AB economy is this: acknowledgement is a shield for imperfection. If we only acknowledged the basketball players who never missed a free throw, no one would be qualified. Those are the best athletes in the world—people who are paid millions of dollars to make baskets—and, when they have a free opportunity with no one blocking them, even *they* miss sometimes.

If we waited to exclusively recognize the parents, teachers, or politicians who have a squeaky-clean record, no one would measure up. But some people don't wait for the Oscars to call their name or the draft to see their value. No matter what trials they might have faced in the past, they find a way to create triumphs in the moment.

Philosopher Bob Jones said, "Acknowledgement is the only way to keep love alive." The NBA slogan is "I love this game." Just think about the type of love it takes to rise to the top of a sport. Olympians will train for years, just for the opportunity to wear a gold medal. The gold medal, itself, that an Olympian puts over their necks is valued at $564.

How could these world-class athletes cherish something like a gold medal that is worth less than $600? It is not about the gold medal. It's about the acknowledgement.

On average, an NBA player's salary is $5.15 million a year. The trophy that they work so hard all season long to earn is valued at $13,500. That means the average player can buy 381 trophies with one year's salary. But it's about the hard work and dedication that it takes to compete against the best in the world and still end up on top. Even the lowest salary player can afford to buy it, but only a few will be acknowledged for earning it.

If you add the cost of all the trophies in all the sports of the world, they would not add up to one million dollars in value, but the acknowledgement that comes with those trophies remains unquantifiable. To this day, great players who earned millions of dollars and did not manage to win a championship feel like they missed out forever.

The average NFL salary is $1.9 million a year. The Lombardi Trophy, made by Tiffany & Co. has a $50,000 value. Each player could afford to purchase 38 trophies, but that would come with no acknowledgement.

Major League baseball is known as America's favorite pastime. On average, MLB players earn $4.2 million a year. The actual commissioner's trophy, however, costs about $15,000. The recognition and acknowledgement from winning the World Series and being a part of the history of an entire league goes beyond the value of silver and gold.

I give you complete permission to crave acknowledgement. It is a joyous occasion when you get the credit for your contribution. Even better when others admit to you how great you are. It's okay to look for that and expect it from others. It could take a long time to learn this. Many people mistake yearning for acknowledgement with not being humble.

You have my unwavering support to seek acknowledgement from people outside of you. To earn their respect. To hear their applause for your talent and ideas. Don't feel bad if your ambition leads you right to the podium, in the middle, where the first-place winner stands.

Keep in mind, however, a gold medal is worth $564. Don't wait until you are surrounded by the press or overwhelmed with customers before you chest-bump yourself.

It is not okay to seek acknowledgement from others if you are not willing to acknowledge yourself. You must start there first. So, before you crave an award, start memorizing your acknowledgement speech. You deserve a blue ribbon right where you are, for *who* you are.

You don't have to be a famous athlete, either. Think of the single mother who works a full-time job while taking classes to further her education. Sometimes, when she is tucking her children in at night, she has to give herself a blue ribbon. She has to learn how to pat herself on the back, even before her children learn the value of her sacrifice. If she doesn't—if she neglects herself for the sake of her child and does not take the time to celebrate her journey—the stress can be unbearable.

What does a military veteran have left after he has been put on medical discharge and physically incapable of fighting for their country? They must learn how to acknowledge their journey, even after the knowledge they have attained becomes irrelevant. Even if they are retired or injured, their journeys will make them warriors for an eternity.

If you took away the Purple Hearts, Stanley Cups, Heisman Trophies, and Lombardi Trophies of the world, there would be no athletic greatness on the global stage. Human beings would not have anything to stretch for.

Acknowledgement strengthens us both ways—when we receive it, *and* when we give it. Right now, I want you to participate in an acknowledgement exercise. The coolest part about the double-edged sword of acknowledgement is that, as far as I know, there is only one truly effective way to give it and receive it at the same time. You will become an expert at this, because the only way to give and receive acknowledgement simultaneously is by acknowledging yourself.

Do not wait on a certificate or a contract. Start right now by listing three things that you really love, and experience the subtle empowerment that this force will lend you.

I want you to write down three things you are really great at doing. But, as you acknowledge your journey, keep in mind it is not limited to time. It's not about *when*, rather, it's more about *what*.

It is so sad that people crave acknowledgement from others, but won't take the time to give it to themselves. The status quo does not have a monopoly on what is considered great. Only *you* can decide if you are good enough to compete and rise to the top, nobody else.

Do not surrender your power of acknowledgement to outside parties. If Oprah calls you and wants to support your book, that is great, but just because Oprah doesn't know your name doesn't mean your book is not worthy of being on the best-seller list. Acknowledgement will shield you from the things about yourself that are not supreme. Don't even think twice about acknowledging the negative parts of you. That is how this power gets abused. Pay more attention to the best of you, and watch the limitations you thought existed disappear.

Yes, acknowledgement is what keeps love alive. But, in the news, they only seem to acknowledge the gossip of the break-up or drama of the day. Acknowledging negativity will make you a great critic, but don't criticize yourself out of a dynasty that only you can produce.

The Talk of Touch

This great force that we call acknowledgement can come in many forms, but there are only three channels through which acknowledgement can be received.

The first of these channels is touch. If you get to touch the trophy, you feel like a champion. To hold the prize in your hands can be an experience that lives within you forever.

When I received a certificate of appreciation from Harvard, I was super-shocked and proud and pumped. The paper can probably be made at Kinko's for less than $5.00, but the experience was priceless. The speech ended, and I was asked to quickly come upstairs, where the press and administrators were waiting. Dean Lambert handed me the certificate and took out a Harvard pin. When I felt the touch on my chest, it felt like the biggest chest-bump ever.

Acknowledgement economics is what drives spectacular team performance. Remember this: touch is a form of communication. When people hold the title in their hands, it feels like it is all worthwhile. Studies indicate that babies who are not touched can suffer from long-term—or even fatal—damage.

Touch is the first language that humans communicate through. It is the most mature form of communication. You might have heard the expression that a picture is worth a thousand words. A touch is worth a thousand pictures.

You can read to a baby all you want. Even show them the best pictures of the world that is waiting for them. If you don't touch them, hug them, and show your love through touch and not just your thoughts, they won't grow. If a newborn goes too long without being touched, they can die.

Life needs touch for sustainability. I remember when my son, Honor, was born. The first thing he touched was my finger. After I cut the cord and said, "You have greatness within you," I picked him up and placed him in his mother's arms.

The doctor taught us that, in the first few weeks, Honor would need skin-to-skin time. There are certain hormones that the mother has within her that he could not get by holding my finger. Those essential nutrients could only be transferred through touch.

When researchers try to figure out why certain orphanages had an infant mortality rate of 30 to 40 percent, they concluded that lack of touch was at the root. These orphans were not being touched. They were not being acknowledged; they could not live on without love.

Touch has been scientifically proven to reduce depression and increase empathy. Touch empathy — as it is called — is a form of communication that we all must learn. Children who are not touched and do manage to survive can grow up to fear making a true bond and connection with others.

I just want to acknowledge that this is my strongest trait as a parent. I love Honor so much; he already knows when daddy is around, it's hug and tickle time. I might eat his little toes or pick him up and spin him in the air. There is nothing like feeling his little hands in my big hands, holding on for dear life.

No one taught me to do that. I just can't help myself. He is the cutest little person I have ever seen. I acknowledge my love for my son through touch.

Through this touch, I communicate to his spirit that I will never abandon him.

Through touch, my son is not just my legacy, but one of my best friends.

Lead the Applause

The first language of acknowledgement is touch. We see the proof of how it impacts children, but many people are mistaken in assuming it is not necessary it is for our entire journey, even into adulthood.

After you go a long time without seeing someone you love, the first thing you do when in their presence is wrap your arms around them and touch their backs.

When it is time to acknowledge a good job, many people will use a high five, communicating the unity between them. How proud they are. Many times, the participants who win an award or a trophy don't get to take it home, but they all get to touch it. Touch is power.

Culturally, across our global landscape, there are many differences that separate us from each other. Beliefs, customs, and race may differ, but it appears that every single culture on earth has chosen to use the same signals of approval when acknowledging massive achievement.

This is a skill that almost everyone has learned without being taught. It instinctively comes out of us in times of awesome. We know that touch is important, because, when we clap our hands, we are giving an acknowledgement-bump to whoever we are clapping for. Our applause is a watered-down version of a blue ribbon, but it sends a message, loud and clear.

When your two hands touch each other, they become what researchers call *articulators*. It makes a sound, without us having to use our voice. A striking of two hands is a universal sign of acknowledgement. However, without two hands touching each other, it is nearly impossible to signal approval in the most common way to do so on Earth.

Here is what we now know about clapping. Number one: we know that it is a universal sign to signal acknowledgment of others. Number two: we expect clapping from others and rely on the acknowledgement of others to validate our approval of ourselves. Number three: if you rely on the acknowledgement and applause of others to acknowledge your journey, you could be waiting forever.

As a graduate in this philosophy, you will learn how to be just as skilled at clapping for yourself as you are at clapping for others. I know it sounds weird, but, after you have your list of three things you love to do, I want you to take at least three minutes out of your day and dedicate one minute per love to acknowledge your journey with touch.

When you touch yourself in a non-sexual, loving way, you are literally acknowledging yourself in a language that your whole body can feel. You are giving acknowledgement and receiving it at the same time. It is okay to crave the attention, but the sequence of craving must have to do with acknowledgement, not just attention. Don't wait for someone else to clap for you. If you are not famous, years can go by without you receiving the touch nutrients that you deserve.

Many people have big goals for the future. Some people want to work towards world peace, or end world hunger. But I just learned of a mission to cure something that is called skin hunger. Have you ever heard of skin hunger? We know that you need food, water, and sleep to live, but skin hunger is a real thing. Skin hunger is a term used to acknowledge the desire that every human be touched. You don't just want to eat; you need to eat to stay alive. The longer you go without it, your body will begin to shut down, whether you realize it or not.

You might find it hard to believe, but there is a whole new industry called professional cuddlers popping up around the world. Massage therapy is just a small fraction of how touch can heal the body. Yet, so many people are malnourished when it comes to positive affection.

Skin hunger is real, but you will use the touching of your own hands as a cure. Science has proven that clapping hands is an activity that stimulates blood flow throughout the entire body. The palms have reflex points that communicate directly with the brain.

I want this semester to inspire you to put the trust back into your own hands by clapping for yourself on a regular basis. You think it's bizarre? Clapping is a language of acknowledgement — acknowledge your journey by thinking of three activities that you love, and lead the applause for you.

Why do people usually clap? It's simple: because others around them are clapping, too. They follow the applause. Sometimes laughing when they don't get the joke or clapping even before they realize who it is for.

When you lead the applause, you don't wait for the others around you to clap before you recognize the power your own two hands. Lead the applause for yourself every day. Don't let one day pass without you acknowledging your journey ever again.

In a controlled group that recorded the claps of 20 different individuals, researchers discovered some interesting facts. Even when all twenty were clapping at the same speed and volume, no two claps were identical. Meaning that there is no other clap in the world that can make the sound that your two hands make when they unite to communicate and articulate.

The fact that most women have smaller hands than men had no impact on the power of the sound. This leads us to our next channel of acknowledgement: sound.

I believe that most people are taught how to be much better at acknowledging others than they are at acknowledging themselves. There is one fatal flaw that keeps us from attaining the power of acknowledgement.

You will never learn how to acknowledge your journey until you unlearn how to compare your journey.

Instead of having a land of acknowledgment experts, we have a land of comparison experts. Many of us are too busy acknowledging somebody else to make time for ourselves.

Have you ever been at a function at which the host asks the audience to give themselves a round of applause for being at the event? Every day, I want you to give yourself a round of applause for showing up in your life. Every day, I want you to think about something that you love doing, that you're really great at, and give yourself a round of applause.

You have the right to believe in you when nobody else does. Brian Tracy coined the term "eve ratio." Your eve ratio is the amount of entertainment vs. education that you consume on a regular basis.

Mr. Tracy did the research and found that, for every fifty minutes of entertainment, the average person only invests about one minute educating themselves. The average "eve ratio" is 50:1.

By the end of a life that lives to be 65 years old, the average person will spend nine years in front of a television screen. What a waste of acknowledgement. Instead of making their own dynasties come true, as soon as they're not working, they watch others live incredible lives, and they call that relaxing.

I think we should also monitor our clap ratio. I think for every 50 minutes we spend acknowledging someone else for how great they are, most people spend less than one minute giving themselves that same love that we all deserve. When you clap for yourself on a regular basis, you will feel the gradual benefits of self-love.

If you're not doing something that's acknowledgment-worthy, you're not doing anything worthwhile. If you give your acknowledgment away to others for too long, without giving it back to yourself, you will suffer from the effects, whether you realize it or not. Acknowledge your journey to avoid dynasty hunger.

Sounds of Success

Sound is the second most effective channel of acknowledgement. To hear a compliment can change how you feel on the inside. As we dig deeper into the sounds of acknowledgement, we must look at the bright side and the dark side.

When someone tells you that you are not good at something, how do you handle that? Look at it for what it is. This is dark side of acknowledgement—nothing more, nothing less. Just as the bright side can empower you, the dark side can incarcerateyou, if you don't know how to handle the sword.

The first time I learned about the dark side was when I decided to pursue a career in the hip-hop music industry. Up until then, I never had to acknowledge my journey, because I got a lot of attention as a public speaker. I received awards and standing ovations and signed autographs, while most kids were only winning in video games. I guess you could say that my childhood was surrounded with acknowledgement.

Then, something different happened in me. I started to look back at my life and all the things I had learned and began to ask questions that I never asked before. I was seized by a restlessness, and I just knew I had to do more with my life than I was doing at the time. I loved music, but I had never heard motivational music being promoted on the radio.

I wanted to share my stories and insight in a world that usually only acknowledges those who glorify violence. I knew that my music could be different. That my voice could be original. The only problem was that it was my journey, no one else's.

Like most dreamers, I tried to convince people of my potential in this new area, but they couldn't see it. I poured my heart out for years, making the music that I had only dreamed of hearing.

I can remember going into the studio, wishing that there was someone to give me a high five. Some type of hidden camera to document my growth. But it was my job. No one high fived me after I made a free throw. No one helped me up after I got fouled.

Somehow, I found a way. Somehow, I made it happen. I listen to motivational music all the time. That is partly how I acknowledge my journey. I let loose in the studio. I pour out everything that I have. It is, by far, my greatest labor of love.

There has been an arsenal of hurtful words released in hip-hop. A ton of acknowledgement about the dark side of society. My music is something else. I really have to acknowledge that, before I did it, I didn't know if I could do it well.

I don't care what anybody says, my music is good. As a matter of fact, it's great. There's only one problem. When people told me I was wasting time and that I would, most likely, fail, it hurt my confidence. After a few years passed without speaking engagements and no applause from others, I thought that maybe I was a has-been.

I started comparing myself to others who were more successful than me in music and thought I would never measure up. Nobody was clapping for my music, and I stopped clapping for myself.

Because of this chapter, I'm going to release my music. When I think about acknowledging my journey, it is the big elephant in the room. I have great music that no one has heard, because I have not been willing to acknowledge its power.

That. Stops. Now!

I let the dark side of acknowledgement hold me back for too long. Follow my lead. What is something that you loved to do, but stopped doing, because you didn't think *others* loved it?

I want you to download my music and think about the elephant in your journey's room that may have been put on the backburner.

Acknowledge your journey, take it off the backburner, and put it on the front burner.

Your second assignment is to listen to motivational music. Music is a form of communication. Positive music can keep you motivated to acknowledge your journey, even when you don't feel up to it.

Everyone has different tastes in music. I love hip-hop. You might love R & B or rock and roll. Regardless, take the time to listen to the music that inspires you. Music that makes you feel more alive.

The right song can give you hope when you think it is lost. Or it can make you want to party. Choose a song that makes you dance, clap, and think at the same time.

You know that sound is a very powerful acknowledgement channel, because when it is truly time to acknowledge something great, we put on music and dance. Dancing is a result of the acknowledgement of sound that you love.

Your second assignment is to dance, dance, dance. Is there a more vulnerable position than the position of being on the dance floor?

Recently, I fell in love and got engaged, and I accompanied my wife -to-be to her class reunion in Lake Charles, Louisiana. After a beautiful day of activities, we ended up at a nightclub.

I like to consider myself a boogie expert. Meaning, when the right music comes on, I know how to boogie. So, that's what we did. As soon as we walked in the building, I reached for my fiancé's hand, and we went straight to the dance floor.

The next day, when some of her friends came to her parents' house, I learned that that's not what people do in Lake Charles, Louisiana. They don't go out to dance, they just go out to profile and look cute. I stood out, big time. One of her friends came by the house and said, "I saw you go all disco fever last night in the club." We all burst into laughter."

The way that you acknowledge your journey will make you stand out. No matter where you go. Just like clapping, dancing is also a universal form of celebration. It is an ancient communication of joy.

It's bigger than just a pat on your back. At least once a week, I want you to find a reason to boogie. Don't be like those people in Lake Charles, Louisiana, who just wanted to profile in their life. If your life is great, show me your moves. Let it all hang out, get your back up off the wall, and turn your steps into dance moves.

Don't let the dark side of acknowledgement stop you from dancing. When you hear a sound that makes you want to move and groove, it can help you deal with the dark side of acknowledgement.

Yes, some people will be rude to you or say no to you. Some might refuse to acknowledge you and may never give you their blue ribbon of approval. Will you let that stop you from moving with joy?

How will you deal with the dark side of acknowledgement? When you hear something negative about yourself, it does not define you. It just reminds you that all acknowledgement is not bright.

However, if you listen to motivational music and dance through their doubt, negative acknowledgement can unleash a force for you in the right direction. The dark side of acknowledgement is put in your life to give you inner momentum.

Music is about inner momentum. So is the dark side of acknowledgement. Don't let one moment of criticism interrupt your momentum. Let it fuel you, not fool you.

It hurt my feelings when some of my closest friends and family didn't like some of my greatest songs, but I never let that stop me from dancing. Now, you will have your own unique motivational catalog of music, and I want you to dance to it.

Even if you're going through a hard time, put my music on and dance. Spoiler alert: you don't just need to acknowledge your journey when everything in your life is looking up. It is even more important that you learn how to acknowledge your journey when everything is looking down. Dancing is a crucial tool that can help us do that.

How often do you dance? I mean *really* dance? Do you know how good it is for your mind, body, and spirit? History teaches us that thousands of years before the written language, dances were used to pass down stories from generation to generation.

Alberto Perlman is someone who has seen how the power of motivational music and dance can change people's lives. At 25 years old, he went to his mother's house for dinner, and she was raving about her new dance classes.

His mom's dance teacher, Beto Perez, had just moved to the United States from Columbia. One day, while still teaching in Columbia, he accidentally forgot his music at home. He went to the car and decided to switch up his lesson, using what he had with him. Hip-hop and salsa, incorporating choreography and powerful uplifting music. His students loved the class that day.

He kept teaching that same class accidental class in America. When Albert heard his mom's happiness and joy about dancing, he knew he had to see it for himself. She told him, "It's the only thing I've ever done that didn't feel like exercise."

When 25-year-old Alberto Perlman visited the class, there were about 150 people in the room of all ages dancing in unity as an exercise. He called his friend, Agion, and approached the instructor with a business deal. Together, the three of them have built the world's number one fitness brand. You might have heard of it. It's called Zumba.

When Alberto went to the class with 150 people in it, it was not called Zumba yet. He had no idea that dance could change the world. He did, however, convince Beto Perez to partner with him and his friend. He knew that if his mom could benefit from it, more people needed access to it. He didn't know at the time that dancing can improve the condition of your heart and lungs, nor that a simple, 60-minute dance can strengthen your endurance, immune system, and motor skills.

Today, over 14 million people take Zumba classes every week. Zumba is taught in over 150 countries, and they have over 140,000 locations worldwide. They say that the secret to the Zumba dynasty is simple. The powerful music that makes the body move. People of all ages take the classes for fun, and it does not feel like exercise to them.

Take care of your body by choreographing your acknowledgement and making a monthly commitment to dance. Dance, even when you feel down. Especially when you feel down. When the dark side of acknowledgement comes your way, dance to regain your strength.

Spend at least 60 minutes a month getting your groove on. You might be amazed at how it makes you feel. Don't just be a profiler in life. Show the world your dance moves, and acknowledge your journey with the power of uplifting music.

Without music that inspires us, we're a danceless people. Joshua Leeds, the author of *The Power of Sound: How to Be Healthy and Productive Using Music and Sound*, teaches people how to use music to reduce stress, enhance learning, and increase productivity. In his must-read book,

Mr. Leeds writes,
> What we hear, and how we process it, has a far greater impact on our daily living than we realize. From the womb to the moment we die we are surrounded by sound, and what we hear can either energize or deplete our nervous systems. It is no exaggeration to say that what goes into our ears can harm us or heal us.

Maybe that is why it is so difficult to take negative acknowledgement with a grain of salt. It's like toxic music to our ears. Some words are so powerful that, once they bounce off our eardrums, become permanently engrained in our memories. Sound and music and memory are the factors that matter when it is time to acknowledge your journey.

Do not let something that gets stuck in your ear cause you to get stuck in your life. When you acknowledge your journey, you are free to get unstuck. You are ready to graduate to the next dimension of your dynasty. When dark music and acknowledgement hit your ear, don't let it knock you down. No matter what you go through on your journey, no matter how high or low it may take you, don't stop dancing.

Researchers discovered how dancing with a partner can influence pain perception. The results were truly amazing. Patients who had a dance partner while listening to music were asked about their level of pain pre-dancing and post-dancing. For the people who danced without a dance partner, their pain level remained the same. However, the pain level of the patients who had someone to dance with decreased dramatically. The results concluded that dancing with a partner to music helps people increase their pain threshold. Even if they have pain, after a good dance, the same pain that they had is no longer perceived the same. Even without the doctors giving them medicine.

Perhaps the most credible evidence that we have about the acknowledgement economy is this. You may think that Wall Street or capitalism is what our economy is all about. Maybe you have become one of those cynical Joe's who thinks that money is at the root of our human culture. Imagine, if you will, what our society would look like if we had no holidays.

The holidays that we celebrate are the ultimate whistle-blowers about the power of acknowledgement vs. knowledge. As Americans, we set aside acknowledgment days at least once a month, and these days represent the most special times of the year.

First, we kick off the year with a New Year's Party. What do people do at these parties? Mostly listen to music and dance. The biggest artists in the world perform the biggest hits of the year. We all stop working and start reflecting about our journeys, while we boogie with each other.

A once-a-year dance off is not enough. It does, however, prove that, instinctively, we know how vital dancing is. It's like that fancy outfit we can't wait to wear, but only wear it on special occasions, like weddings, graduations, or parties.

After New Year's Day, the next big holiday is Dr. Martin Luther King Jr.'s birthday. A whole day is set aside to acknowledge the journey of one great

American, who said, "We must accept finite disappointment, but never lose infinite hope."

The next one, Valentine's Day, is to acknowledge love. Then, it's President's Day, to acknowledge political leadership. After that, we have Black History Month, Columbus Day, Mother's Day, Father's Day, Memorial Day, Independence Day, and Labor Day. Let's not forget Thanksgiving, and, last but not least, comes December. We go all-out with acknowledgement during Christmas.

As Americans, we recognize that there is enough acknowledgement to go around for everybody. It is part of our culture, because it makes us clap our hands, give gifts, and dance with one another.

Acknowledge your journey, even if it is not your birthday or some major holiday. Listen to upbeat music, and use as many positive words as you can.

The main benefit of honoring yourself with dance and applause is that these activities are major stress-reducers. Let's face it, every life is a journey, and, within that journey can be some bright times and some dark times. The dark times can leave us stressed out. Stress is no good for the body.

Fortunately, acknowledgement with positive words can be the cure for much of the stress that we all must face on our journey. According to the book *Words Can change your Brain*, certain positive words, if focused on ten to twenty minutes a day, have the power to influence genetic expression in your brain.

Herbert Benson's team at the Massachusetts Boston Hospital found that, "The repetition of purposely meaningful words can actually turn on stress-reducing genes." The motivational music that you will dance to will trigger the genes that relieve stress.

Wouldn't it be great to have a strategy of what to do whenever you get stressed out? Imagine how much more powerful you would feel if you had a firm strategy about what to do when people say things about you that make you feel sick to your stomach?

Now, you have a strategy. Acknowledge your journey. Don't wait for someone else to have a party for you or applaud for you. Lead the applause for yourself. Make your own theme music about your life and dance your way to your dynasty. You deserve it.

You are a graduate of the H.A.R.V.A.R.D. Effect .

RISE TO THE OCCASION

> *"The occasion is piled high with difficulty, and we must rise with the occasion. As our case is new, so we must think anew and act anew."*
> -Abraham Lincoln

Now is time to act. Calling all high-achievers. Calling all leadership warriors. I need your help. This journey we call life does not always signal when it is time to move with a sense of urgency and seize the moments that we are given. With your help, *The H.A.R.V.A.R.D. Effect* can set a new standard of success.

A standard that is not about where you graduate, rather, what you are graduating *with*.

You have a hundred-year plan. You have a long-term agenda for your purpose. There are a lot of new ideas to digest. Be aware that, as you live out this effect, it will create opportunities that you might not have ever anticipated. Do not be too shy to enjoy your special occasion.

Rise up, ye mighty people. Alberto Perez was just 25 years old when he walked into his mother's dance class. Some people would have seen it as a joke or a waste of time. Other sons might not have even visited the dance class with his mother. Alberto not only went to the class, but because he saw that moment as an occasion he is now the CEO of a multi-billion-dollar dance fitness company.

Think about what would have happened if there was no Zumba. If Alberto did not add his team and expertize to help over 14 million people weekly with dance. Can you imagine if Zumba was just some unnamed work-out group in just one local community? It's hard to fathom that now, because, at just 25 years old, Alberto Perez decided to rise to the occasion.

I want you to know that there is a special occasion for your life. I'm not talking about your birthday. I mean an occasion that is specially carved out for you. Nobody else can rob you of your occasion but you. It is yours. It belongs to you. It has been waiting for you all along.

This occasion will not be given to you. You're going to have to earn it. You are going to have to work for it, and learn for it, and cry for it, and fight for it. But, once you arrive at this occasion that I describe, you will forever be transformed. Others will be at the same event that you are attending, but your experiences will be totally unique.

I recently had a rise-to-the-occasion moment when I met the woman of my dreams. I have traveled the world and met a lot of beautiful people, but, when I walked into the Billboard Awards after party in Las Vegas, this beautiful soul caught my eye. There she stood, my dream woman, a few feet away from me. Even before I approached her, I instantly knew that, if I could get to know her better, she might be the one.

You know it is time to rise to the occasion when you think to yourself, *This might be the one.* This might be the one relationship or phone call or community project that is perfectly suited for you.

When I approached the most beautiful woman that I had ever laid eyes on, I knew that I would have one shot at making her mine. One shot at taking her out on a date and pulling out my greatest gentleman. I knew even before I offered to buy her a drink that, if I was going to get to know a woman as beautiful as she, it was going to require me to be a better man than I had been in any other relationship.

You want to always look for people and opportunities that demand you to be better than you have been before. I have never been the type of guy to avoid talking to a woman, just because she's beautiful. When faced with the opportunity of a lifetime, some people sit back and make excuses about who they could have been or what they might have done.

I saw a chance to talk to the most gorgeous woman in the room, and I took it.

Fortunately for me, it was my birthday, and I was feeling and looking great. The Billboard Music Awards had just ended, and, needless to say, Drai's Nightclub had a star-studded crowd. One woman, however, immediately caught my attention as my friends and I came through the door.

When something catches your attention, give it a shot, even if your chances are unknown. I asked the most beautiful woman I have ever seen if I could get her a drink, and, then, we started to chat a little. While we were talking for the first time, I remember thinking, *Oh my greatness, she is beautiful and intelligent.* When she told me she was a director and actress, I just knew that I was in the presence of a rising star.

At that precise moment, one of my friends tapped me on the back and whispered in my ear, "Get her number, man, and let's go. There are a lot of beautiful women in here." I wasn't man enough to say no. I asked her for her number, and, when she agreed and asked for my phone, so she could enter her number, in my mind, it was like winning the World Series. For some reason, she stood out to me. I spent the rest of the night searching the club, just to find her again. I was unsuccessful. I thought that if I could just have one dance with her, it would mean more than dancing with every other woman in the room.

The good news was that I had her number. The bad news was that she saved it in my phone, and, because I did not remember her name, I could not find her number among my other 632 contacts. I was so upset. I could not even call her to see if the number she gave me was real. There was only one thing left for me to do. I had to rise to the occasion.

I went through my 632 contacts one by one, until, finally, I came across an unfamiliar name, and I googled it. It turns out Taja V. Simpson was real, not just a figment of my imagination. We began dating, and this woman quickly inspired me to rise to the occasion of marriage.

Sometimes, I used to wonder if true love existed. If I could ever find it. When I finally found it, it made me pull out a side of myself that I knew was there, but had never paid attention to. For me, rising to the occasion meant getting down on one knee. On a beautiful cruise ship in Hawaii, I orchestrated the proposal of a lifetime, because I wanted our engagement to be unforgettable.

It was tough picking out a ring and, then, hiding it for the whole trip. I had to acknowledge my journey in relationships and ask myself if I was truly ready to be a husband. To provide for and protect the woman of my dreams. That answer was yes. My question for you is this. When life throws a once-in-a lifetime opportunity your way, what will your answer be?

Up On Bended Knee

The day of our engagement was her birthday. I love the fact that we met on my birthday and got engaged on hers. I wanted the entire day to be special and exciting, so I decided to get her surfing lessons that morning. Neither of us had surfed before, but I thought she would enjoy surfing on Waikiki Beach in Honolulu.

There was only one problem: as I listened to the surfing instructor telling us how to stand up on the board, it suddenly dawned on me that he expected us to surf in just one session. Meaning that same day. Now, the birthday girl was excited, but, to be honest, I was thinking, *I really don't want to die before I pop the big question.*

The instructor, Chris, was a Hawaiian native and looked like he grew up surfing. He explained how we had to stay in our own lane and swim on top of the boards with our stomachs flat, using our arms to paddle. He warned us that it may be exhausting, reminding us that we would be swimming against the tide. If we stopped to take a breath, the momentum would take us backwards.

After we reached a certain distance, we would regroup, and, one at a time, he would set us up to ride a wave. When the wave came, we were to lay flat on our board, until the fastest point of momentum pushed us forward. Then, we were to push up with our arms, and get up on bended knee.

As he described this, I wanted to pull him aside and say, "Chris, tonight, I am going to propose to this woman, and I really don't want to die or get bitten by a shark before or after that happens, so can you go without me?" The only problem was that, as a man, I was too afraid to let the woman of my dreams know how afraid I was.

I said, "Chris, you sound very confident. Do you really expect us to stand up on the board today?" He chuckled and replied, "Yes. If you can walk from here to the beach, you can stand on the board. Follow all my instructions, and you are going to stand up on the board today."

My voice got a little shaky, and I began to feel weak in the knees. If it weren't for the gorgeous woman that I was so in love with, there was no way that I would have been surfing.

I might stick my feet in the water, maybe, but never surf. That was not something that was in my hundred-year plan. I knew she would be surprised and that it would be fun for her, but, when I purchased the lessons I thought it would take a few weeks to get up on the board, and that, at this first lesson, we could just kind of paddle out and sit on the boards. I thought we would stand on the boards in the sand, but I never would have agreed to it, had I been by myself.

I asked, "Chris, is this dangerous?"

He had a straight face, but I thought he was joking. "Yes, surfing is dangerous. If you fall off your board, make sure you use both your arms to cover your head. There will be other surfers in the water, and their boards can hit your head and hurt you. Also, if you don't protect yourself, your own board can bump your head and knock you out. And, remember, the rocks at the bottom of the ocean are very sharp in Waikiki. It's not sand out there, so make sure you stay on your board as much as you can."

I remember thinking to myself, *If I just run away right now and go up to the hotel room and lock the door, there's no way she will say yes when I propose later tonight.* I asked if I could use the bathroom, but the truth is I did not have to use the bathroom. I had to look in the mirror and make a choice:

> A) *This would be a perfect time to go back to the hotel room, maybe if I turn off my phone, she will just come back after the lesson is over.*

B) *I could use the H.A.R.V.A.R.D. Effect and rise to the occasion.*

I couldn't let my fears of drowning, bumping my head, and getting eaten by sharks interfere with the love of my life. I had to rise to the occasion.

I didn't go back to the hotel room, like I wanted to. I went back to the class, where the instructor finished telling me how to go from standing up on bended knee, to standing up all the way on a surfboard.

After you have that knee planted in the right place, as that momentum starts to pull you along and the board is moving faster than you've felt it move before, there is only one thing left to do. Rise.

Maybe you know what it feels like to be up on bended knee. Maybe you know what it's like to position yourself to stand atop a wave. As you receive your master's degree in the H.A.R.V.A.R.D. Effect, you will become flexible, vertical, and adaptable. There was a time when performance could remain at the same level, and people could expect to get the same results. Today, however, we must constantly elevate beyond who we have been to maintain what we used to have. The 16th. U.S. President put it best when he said, "The dogmas of the quiet past are inadequate to the stormy present."

I had to talk to myself as a man and let go of the fears that I used to have as a boy. As a master of the H.A.R.V.A.R.D. Effect, I urge you not to just make a hundred-year plan and continue living life the same as you were a hundred days ago. Every idea you have that might feel beyond you right now, but it doesn't mean that you are not good enough to reach it. It just means you know that what you are doing today is not what can get you there tomorrow. Rise up.

I knew that this new relationship would require me to stand taller than I had ever stood. But, before I could get down on one knee and pop the question, I had a question that I had to answer for myself. It is the same question I want you to consider as you near the conclusion of your mastery of this effect:

What occasion are you rising to?

Chris, our surfing mentor, handed us huge boards. As I lifted the colorful, risky toy above my head, to balance it for the walk to the shore, my heart began to beat faster. I could feel the fear throughout my body.

Then, Chris shared the final rule of the water. This one rule, forced me to rise to the occasion. "Everyone who gets into the water together is going to be getting out of the water together. If someone gets tired or wants to leave, everybody has to get out."

Now the pressure was on. I could not let my cowardice ruin the birthday of the woman I love. When we finally reached Waikiki Beach, the water was a lot warmer than I thought. I began swimming atop my board, against the tide. I quickly noticed that, out of the four of us, I was moving the slowest. It almost seemed like, even though my arms were just as long as everybody else's, they just didn't work as well in the water.

That is when the humiliation started. Our mentor, Chris, saw me falling behind everyone else, and he swam back to me. He said, "I can see that you're a little tired already. Just hold on to the board; I'll take you the rest of the way." Then, he turned around and I saw his toe latch onto the tip of my board. I thought to myself, *Is he about to drag me out to sea with his toe?*

I could not believe it. He was able to pull himself and me in the water faster just than I could pull just myself using my arms, using one of his big toes. I just hoped that nobody noticed. It would have been hard to miss.

Before I even got dragged to where the waves were, I had been ready to quit. Love was the only thing that kept me going. Looking back, I must acknowledge that.

The occasion that I was rising to had nothing to do with surfing. I was rising to the occasion of love. Whatever it is that you love to do — whether it is acting, speaking, or marketing — commit to your love.

Life has many events we must attend. Not all of them are special. Our most precious events are not called events. Our most precious events are called occasions. Love is one of life's best occasions. It doesn't appear by just loving someone else. The highest form of love is self-love.

Will you love yourself enough not to let yourself down again and again: Do you trust yourself enough to be vulnerable, even if it means you must risk getting your heart broken? What occasion are you rising to?

There's an old surfer's quote that says, "Waves are inspiring, not because they rise and fall, but because they never fail to rise again." That day on the beautiful waves on Waikiki Beach, I rose to the occasion.

Are you ready to rise? You might be feeling like you're moving too slow.

Let me latch my big toe around your "self-board," and I will drag you to where you are too afraid to go by yourself.

The first key to rising to the occasion is flexibility. You must be flexible if you want to live on the cutting edge. That's where we can find the waves. For this, I want you to find a Chris. Find someone who can mentor you in an area that you love. Someone who cares enough about you not to leave you when you feel like you are falling behind.

Flexibility requires big toes and small egos. As he dragged me to the area with Mike—another first-time student in our class, who about 20 years older than me—and Taja—the love I was trying to impress—I had to let go of my shame and fear and rely on my mentor's instructions.

When it's time to rise to the occasion, who do you call? Ron Biles, an air traffic controller from Texas decided to call on his wife when faced with a rise-to-the-occasion moment. Ron had a daughter from a previous marriage who had gotten addicted to drugs and alcohol. This challenge made it impossible for her to take proper care of her four kids. She lost custody of them, and they were living in a foster home.

Ron and his wife, Nellie, had already raised two boys who were entering college, and in their late 40s, neither Ron nor Nellie planned on taking full custody of toddlers.

When he got the call from the social worker, he chose to rise to the occasion. He asked his wife one question that would one day change Olympic history. "Would it be possible for us to take them in?" Then, he said three words that should never be forgotten: "They need us."

This chapter is crucial, because now, more than ever, we need you. Some people allow their journeys in life to be a reason to get jaded about the future. Because of that, life becomes predictable. This unpredictable, unfortunate family matter would change history books forever.

Ron Biles had to be flexible to ask his wife that question. He and his wife took full responsibility and made the necessary lifestyle adjustments to become full-time parents again.

They raised their two grandchildren as if they were their own daughters. They rose to the occasion as a team. If it was not for their love and guidance, the world's greatest female gymnast, might not have ever learned her full potential.

They took in two of their granddaughters, Simone and Shanon. Simone Biles had been in a foster home that had a big trampoline in the backyard, but, because she was only three years old, she was never allowed to use it.

Despite her tough start in life, Ron Biles's granddaughter has gone on to win 19 Olympic and world championship gold medals. She is the most decorated Olympian in the world, at 19 years old. Journalists and experts are amazed at what Simone Biles can do as a gymnast. Knowing her real-life journey puts me in awe of Mr. Ron Biles and what he was able to do as a grandfather.

He asked the right question to the right person. To rise to the occasion, you are going to need to ask the right question to the right person. That is what precedes a worthy occasion. The right question.

When I was in the waters of Waikiki Beach, I was challenged way beyond my comfort zone. Taja, the woman of my dreams, had picked up surfing instantly and was having the time of her life. Me, on the other hand… let's just say I kept falling off my board when it was time to rise.

For some reason, even the other gentleman—who was at least twenty years older than me—could ride up on his board multiple times. I still remember feeling embarrassed. Everyone was having fun, but me. Taja would breeze by me with a big smile on her face, like a surfing ninja, riding every wave that came her way. At first, I was cheering her on, but, eventually, even that got exhausting. I was just ready to get out of the water.

Then, I asked the right question to the right person. Chris, our instructor, had given us those instructions before we had even reached the water. Even though I thought I was following them, I just could not rise up. For me, it meant more than not riding a wave, it meant that the woman of my dreams would not see a side of me that I had never seen.

A side of me that is willing to try something new. A part of me that was willing to rise to the occasion, no matter what it may be. I just wanted to do it for the woman I loved. So she could be proud of me. So that, years later, we can say, "On the day of our engagement, we surfed on Waikiki Beach."

It was almost time for our session to be over, and Chris pulled me back out to the wave with his big toe, once again. This time, he looked at me and said, "Ananaho."

I asked him what it meant, and, with infinite hope, he looked at me and said, "the last wave."

Above the Wave

I looked at my future wife, and I asked her a question. I had to acknowledge my journey and hers. She got the hang of it, and I didn't. This was her first time, too.

Why is it that she was rising to the occasion, and I wasn't? I asked her, "What's your secret?"

She looked at me with a straight face and said, "I followed the instructions."

I thought she was being sarcastic. Then, I thought about it again. The whole time I was in the water, I was too busy trying not to drown or bump my head. I totally forgot the instructions that we got from Chris. The air traffic in my own mind prevented me from rising up into the air.

The last wave was before me, and I realized that the whole time I was in the water, I was not following the instructions I had been given on land. If you really want to rise to the occasion, remember all you must do is ask the right question to the right person.

A new occasion requires a new question. The kind that Ron asked his wife when he asked, "Is it possible for us to take them in?" I don't think he was a just asking his wife, I'm certain he was asking himself, as well. Because they were flexible, their sacrifice as grandparents will never vanish from the pageless history books.

This time, on the last wave, I pushed up to bended knee, and, for the first time in my life, I rose up on a surfboard. With joy and disbelief, I felt the water pulling me faster than ever. "Ananaho!"

Suddenly, all the other surfers around us started cheering and screaming out, "Ananaho. You did it, you did it." They saw me fall off the board again and again. On the last wave, in front of a wet crowd and the love of my life, I rose to the occasion.

Whenever you make the choice to rise, remember that you need a mentor or a coach you will actually listen to. We all have a lot of air traffic in our minds. Your mentor is someone who can serve as an air traffic controller.

I live in Los Angeles, California, where, amongst being known for many things—like Hollywood and palm trees—we are known to have the worst traffic in the country. When I visit other cities and listen to them complain about traffic, I laugh. They haven't seen traffic until they have been on the 405 Freeway.

On the ground, people will do anything to avoid the traffic. They wake up several hours earlier than necessary and try to find creative routes, but, if you live in L.A., there is no way to avoid the traffic. If you think ground traffic is bad, wait until you experience air traffic.

Visual observation is the only thing standing in the way of you rising to the occasion every time. Some people get so frustrated with life that they would not recognize a rise moment if it was standing right in front of them. Their visual observations of what is behind them get in the way.

You can't look at how difficult something is going to be and allow that to deter you from your occasion. Fear has no place in your future. Ron Biles was an air traffic controller, so he knew how to master the art of visual observations.

It's unimaginable what you can accomplish when you overcome the fear of your journey. But, just because you rise to the occasion doesn't mean that you get to skip around the traffic in life. No matter what time you take off or how creative you get with your flight path, you are bound to run into air traffic.

Air traffic clouds the ideas floating in your head with other people's visual observation of what they expect of you.

My fiancée helped me to navigate through the air traffic in my head. She became the mentor for me that reminded me that I knew what it took to rise. Who's going to help you control your air traffic?

When I rose up on that board, I was too shocked to look at Taja's face, but I faintly heard her cheers in the distance. It was amongst a lot of cheers that I did not anticipate. I didn't realize all the people who were watching on our journey there, in the water. Just as you have no idea who is watching you on your journey of life. When you rise to the occasion and complete something you once bought was beyond you, you will be drowned with acknowledgement from all directions.

Remember, just because you make it to the next level doesn't mean you get to coast. I still had to maintain my balance on the board. Do you have all the support you need to rise to the occasions that triggers unknown passions within you?

Be flexible. Don't become an old dog who hates new tricks. When I had the pleasure of sharing this message with the students and faculty at Harvard, I knew I had risen to the occasion.

Throughout my career, I had given the same speech. I was sharing what I learned as a boy, but not what I have mastered as man.

After it was over, I knew that the real work had just begun. I knew I need to share the same message that I shared at Harvard with you. This book has been an occasion for me. I didn't know if I could do it, just like Ron and Nellie were not certain that they could raise their granddaughters. But I did it, they did it, and so will you.

Rise up, ye mighty achiever. You were born to contribute. Keep rising up. Stop reading your own biography, and start rewriting with your new agenda.

Yes, there is traffic. Yes, you will experience turbulence. Yes, it might be risky or dangerous. Yes, you will have to make many sacrifices. Most importantly, *yes*, you *can* rise to the occasion. When you do, you'll never look down on yourself again.

How are we going to heal a society in which one in three people are diagnosed with cancer? We need some new medical minds to rise. How will we go on with toxic political discourse that leaves little time to discuss the real issues? We need more political scientists to rise now.

Whether it's protecting our environment, serving our country, or launching a non-profit organization that makes lasting change, you can rise to the occasion.

Get ready, as a H.A.R.V.A.R.D. Effect graduate: more opportunities will be recognizable. Be flexible with your expectations of yourself, so that you don't miss out on an opportunity that can alter your path forever.

Sometimes, rising to the occasion is knowing when to say yes. Often, rising to the occasion is knowing when to say no. If you know within your heart that an opportunity is not for you, don't compromise your values. The right occasion will find you, just be open to your progress. If you don't rise to the occasion, you can be stuck in the same journey forever.

Call to Elevation

I said no to everything else in my life besides this book. This became my single focus. I only ask that you remember this is not an assignment that you turn in, its an assignment that you turn out. Rise to the occasion by teaching this effect to your most valued loved one. Share the ideas from this book, and become a H.A.R.V.A.R.D. Effect professor.

The quickest way to rise to the occasion is to lift someone else up. Sometimes, rising does not mean that you will be in the spotlight. Sometimes, it means that you will be there for someone wjp is. Your one thesis assignment is to become a mentor. Latch your big toe to someone else's board.

I plan to share the H.A.R.V.A.R.D. Effect with middle school students and toddlers, preparing them for high achievement at an early age. Reminding them that they are bright enough to cast out the darkness in the world. Will you join me? Rise to the occasion, and make sure that the H.A.R.V.A.R.D. Effect is never forgotten. Bring the action steps on the pages to life by sharing this with your community.

Become the air traffic controller for someone else, and watch how swiftly you rise to the occasion. The best things that you do in life will not be measured on how high they elevate you, they are measured by how high you elevate others. Those journeys are the ones that deserve the most acknowledgement.

Congratulations, you are now a participant in the H.A.R.V.A.R.D. Effect. The following chapter is your final step for graduating from the elite motivational university that I have spent a lifetime learning. There is only one final frontier to master. I'm sure you will not be disappointed when you apply these principles in your life.

DWELL IN GRATITUDE

*Gratitude is not only the greatest of virtues
but the parent of all others.*
-Cicero

Thank you. I am so grateful to share this experience with you. I have never really shared all that I wanted to from the stage. I have learned a lot. I wasn't sure if I had something truly powerful to offer the world, until I started writing this book. It is my firm belief that all the ideas and stories that I have shared with you can make a difference in your life. But, even if you complete every semester, but skip this critical level, you are doing yourself a disservice.

A few years ago, I learned about a seminar being held by Jairek Robbins. I was transformed by his insights, and thought I was ready to apply them. We became friends, and, one day, I called him while I was going through a tough financial time.

He asked me a question that truly taught me about who he was as a man and inspired me to be a better coach. He asked, "What are three things you are grateful for?" I was a little taken aback, because I felt like maybe he was being insensitive to my complaints. Then, I remembered something that I will never forget. Gratitude is more important than gratuity.

At the end of the day, we all face setbacks and upsets that can affect our finances. That is understandable, but your gratitude should never be in debt. Be grateful for everything and everyone that truly matters to you. Don't take anything or anyone for granted. Every day, I want you to ask the right person the right question. The right person is you. The right question is the question that Jairek asked me. What are three things that you are grateful for?

In our society, it is a known fact that bad news travels faster than good news. We are more prone to pick up the phone and tell all the details about a bad day than we are about a great one. In the book *Buddha's Brain*, it talks about how bad news is stored differently in the brain than good news. It likens the brain to Velcro for good news and Teflon for bad news.

Let's just face it, bad news happens. The challenge, therefore, lies in not avoiding bad news, rather, the biggest challenge is not to dwell on bad news. That is a big mistake people make. Focusing on the wrong for way too long. That is why it takes numerous positive experiences to undo one negative experience, but only one negative experience to undo several positive ones.

Despite how your memories are stored differently in the hippocampus, put your gratitude to the test, and see if you can become as good at spreading great news as most people are at sharing tragedy.

Sympathy is a natural desire for everybody. Sometimes, when we are sharing tragedy, we know we can overcome it, but we want others to sympathize with us. Unfortunately, sympathy cannot make you rich. Sympathy will not inspire people to help you. You cannot dwell in gratitude if you are digging for sympathy.

Gratitude is never invited to a pity party. It looks at pity the way most people look at poverty. When a person is in poverty, it appears that they are missing out on the best that life has to offer. What most people don't realize is that sympathy and poverty are interconnected.

When you complain to people about how poor your finances are, it only makes you poorer. When you seek sympathy from people and complain about how bad things are, that only makes it worse. Sympathy and poverty go hand-in-hand, just like gratitude and wealth.

Nobody sympathizes with the wealthy. They are too busy dwelling in admiration or envy. From this semester forward, make sympathy your enemy and gratitude your ally.

We cannot control what happens in life, but we *can* control the thoughts we dwell on. Your final assignment is to dwell in gratitude every day. I want you to make a gratitude savings account and, for 365 days, deposit checks addressed to causes and people you are grateful for. There is just one catch: it has to be two things you are grateful for, and one thing that hasn't even happened yet that you plan to be grateful for in the future.

For gratitude to be truly unlimited, sometimes, it must be preemptive. Preemptive gratitude will be a tough, but important, state of mind. Keep your thoughts pointed at the appreciation of the occasions to come.
In 1848, James W. Marshal became the first to discover gold in California. The following year, the good news had spread so far and wide that there was gold in the Golden State that 100,000 people relocated, giving birth to the term 49er. By 1849, the Gold Rush had begun. People started moving to California with the thoughts of walking down the street and picking up gold nuggets, just like James W. Marshal.

All because they heard some good news. They expected to find gold, and they moved at the thought of a fortune. Your fortune does not require you to go anywhere, but it *does* require you to dig deep inside you and recognize the gold that is within you.

The Gold Rush

Perhaps the ones who have mastered gratitude the most are the people who have the fewest material possessions. Gratitude has very little to do with what you have on the outside, but everything to do with how are you feeling inside.

Jane Ransom once said, "Gratitude is gold." We all know that the dollar bill is just a promissory note. Many years ago, money was backed by gold. Now, it is not backed by gold; it is backed by gratitude.

What good is it to be the richest man in the world, if you are depressed? Can you really enjoy your sports car if it costs you your peace of mind? Let gratitude be your new monetary system.

Sometimes, it feels like everyone is out to get rich. But true wealth only comes your way when you are grateful for what you have, even if you don't have a lot.

You will have a lot in your dynasty. Things will come and go in this semester, and I want to make sure that your gratitude is here to stay. Even for the things that have not happened yet.

Most people have only been taught one way to show gratitude. They rely on a thank you. Go the extra mile and make a ritual of writing out checks of gratitude. Go to your bank and get a checkbook.

At the beginning of the day, write out a check, and assign a dollar amount. The check should be addressed to gratitude from your past. At the end of the day, before you go to sleep, write out two more checks. One for your present day, and one for your future gratitude. Keep these in a safe or a private hidden area. Let them build up for 365 days. Look at it like a gratitude savings account.

Gratitude keeps you rich. At the end of this 365-day journey, I want you to review your gratitude account. America is the wealthiest nation on earth, but we also are the most wasteful. We represent only five percent of the world's land, but our waste takes up 30 percent. We have the abundance to throw away the most trash, but let's make sure that we never waste our gratitude.

File for Thankruptcy

When a person has too much debt to pay back, sometimes, they make the choice to file for bankruptcy. It is a term that many of us have heard, but few of us really understand. After filing for bankruptcy, it does not eliminate your debt, but it allows you to make smaller payments to pay it back.

Millions each year file for bankruptcy. The number one cause for bankruptcy in America is the cost of medical bills. People who must use all their money to get the care and medicine they need to stay alive. I want you to file for thank-ruptcy. Write out checks of gratitude every day for one whole year, and, at the end of that year, read each gratitude note to one of the people you are grateful for. Let them know how meach they mean to you. File for thank-ruptcy, and let the people you are indebted to them.

This will open a vault of wealth in your life. I love the quote that says, "Never let what you want, cause you to forget what you have."

Write a check out to your body, and put a pricetag of gratitude that you have for your legs. Write a check out to your parents, and put a pricetag on what their love has meant to you. Write a check of gratitude every day, and, at the end of one year, file for thank-ruptcy. Watch your gratitude build up. A lot of us waste our gratitude, because we get overwhelmed by all the debt. There are so many who help up along the way that it is almost overwhelming to keep track.

For example, for my speech at Harvard to take place, I cannot take all the credit. As a matter of fact, most the credit goes to other people. If it were not for Ona Brown, Mamie Brown, Les Brown, Lajaune Bryant, Dolly Amaya, and Berny Dhorman, the event would have never taken place. Six people were needed just for one event.

If you plan to leave behind a dynasty, you are going to have to make a choice to be rich in gratitude. You will go into major debt if your hundred-year plan is brought to life. When you let people know how grateful you are for them, you will live in their hearts forever. This is the smaller form of payment that you can give.

Let them know how grateful you are for them and why.

Ona Brown, I am grateful for you for managing the contract and relationship with Harvard University. When it appeared as if the event would be cancelled, you kept the faith. You told me to hold the vision and get ready for an opportunity of a lifetime. I struggled for weeks about the content of the speech, but at the last minute, you gave me all the points that I am writing about in *The H.A.R.V.A.R.D. Effect*. You are the greatest professor, sister, coach, and dancer. I love you, sis. This entire project would not be possible without the way you show your love for me. I am grateful.

Mamie Brown, you are what my speech was about. That is what the Harvard Effect is about. Mamie Brown embodies these principals. Her flesh is no longer here, but my gratitude for her dynasty is never extinct. Thank you, Mamie Brown, for adopting my dad, and teaching him, the H.A.R.V.A.R.D. Effect.

Les Brown and Lajaune Bryant, you two dynamic parents belong in the parental hall of fame. Dad, you showed up for me at Harvard that day. You sat in the front row, and I am grateful for what you said after the speech. You taught me everything I know. I love you, and I am grateful that you paved the way for me in this industry. Thank you.

Mommy, you were my speaker coach even before I was born. You always see the best in me and expect the best *from* me. Your love and guidance and watching the way you read and study inspired me to pull out my best. I love you, Ma. Next time I go to Harvard, I'm taking you with me.

Dolly Amaya, thank you for taking Berny Dhorman's recommendation and for giving my voice a chance. Thank you for getting behind this book project. You are now an alumni of the H.A.R.V.A.R.D. Effect.